THE VIOLET DOTS

THE

VIOLET DOTS

BY

MICHAEL KERNAN

GEORGE BRAZILLER

NEW YORK

Published in the United States in 1978 by George Braziller, Inc.
Copyright © 1978 by Michael Kernan

The author gratefully acknowledges permission to reprint his material which originally appeared in the June 27, 1976 and June 22, 1977 issues of *The Washington Post*. Reprinted by permission of *The Washington Post*.

Library of Congress Cataloging in Publication Data

Kernan, Michael, 1927–
   The violet dots.

   1. Easton, Tom. 2. Northumberland, Eng.—
Biography. I. Title.
CT788.E23K47   942.8'8'0820924 [B]   77–94496
ISBN 0–8076–0887–4

Printed in the United States of America
FIRST EDITION

To Nathan, Lisa and Nicholas

and

To Margot

ACKNOWLEDGMENTS

Clearly, this book owes a great deal to serious historians and others who have devoted much time to the Somme and World War I, but most of all it is indebted to Martin Middlebrook, the man who introduced me to Tom Easton in the first place.

Middlebrook, who interviewed over five hundred people in a labor of love inspired by a visit to the British cemeteries on the Somme, is a source without equal for an account of 1 July 1916 and for the Somme battle in general. His work, *The First Day on the Somme,* is also rich in insights about the war itself, how the generals viewed it, how the privates felt about it, how they changed.

For a first-rate impressionistic account of the young officer in that war, I recommend Robert Graves' *Goodbye to All That,* which combines the immediacy of a diary with the irony of an intelligent memoir.

I am grateful to the Departments of Documents and Printed Books at the Imperial War Museum, London, for making available to me a number of unpublished records in their care (including the unpublished diaries of Captain Reginald Leetham, Lieutenant Kenneth Macardle, Edward G. D. Liveing, and an anonymous German survivor of the Somme), and to Mr. D. F. Macardle for permission to quote from the diary of his brother, Lieutenant Kenneth Macardle, which is now lodged in the Museum's Department of Documents.

Permission has been received, and is gratefully acknowledged, from the following authors and publishers, to reproduce quotations and extracts as follows:

A. R. Griffin, *Coalmining* (Essex: Longman, 1971), pp. 132–136. Copyright © A.R. Griffin, 1971. Reprinted by permission of Penguin Books Ltd.

Martin Middlebrook, *The First Day on the Somme* (London: Penguin, 1971). By permission of Martin Middlebrook and Allen Lane Ltd.

George Coppard, *With a Machine-Gun to Cambrai* (London: Her Majesty's Stationery Office, 1969). Reproduced with the permission of the Controller of Her Britannic Majesty's Stationery Office.

Georges Blond, *Verdun, 1916* (Deutsch, 1966).

John Laffin, *Surgeons in the Field* (London: J. M. Dent, 1970). By permission of John Laffin.

Philip Gibbs, *The Realities of War* (London: Hutchinson, 1929). Reproduced by permission of Curtis Brown Ltd., London, on behalf of the Estate of Sir Philip Gibbs.

From *The Times History of the War*, Vol. IX (London: Times Publishing Co., 1916).

From *In Flanders Fields* by Leon Wolff. Copyright © 1958 by Leon Wolff. Reprinted by permission of The Viking Press.

Robert Graves, *Goodbye to All That* (New York: Double-day, 1957). By permission of Robert Graves.

Norman Gladden, *The Somme, 1916* (London: William Kimber, 1974).

Christopher Martin, *Battle of the Somme* (London: Wayland, 1973).

John Temple, *Mining: An International History* (London: Ernest Benn, 1972).

Robert Graves and Alan Hodge, *The Long Week-End* (New York: Norton, 1963). By permission of Robert Graves.

Quoted from *Northumberland Heritage* by Nancy Ridley by permission of the Publishers, Robert Hale Limited, London.

Northumberland County Handbook (London: Edward J. Burrow).

Donald R. Morris, *Washing of the Spears* (London: Sphere Books, 1973).

There is also, of course, William Reiss, my agent, who never gave up.

THE VIOLET DOTS

July first, 1916: On paper it looked so good that ailing soldiers lied their way out of the hospitals just to be a part of this Big Push on the Somme.

The British generals were so sure of at last breaking the trench stalemate that they had three divisions of cavalry waiting behind the lines to overrun the German rear and spill out across northern France to reach the sea and end the war itself. Even the British people at home knew about the plan many weeks ahead, and a speech by a member of Parliament which nicely bracketed the expected starting date was published in newspapers available to the Germans.

It was General Sir Douglas Haig who had the dream about the cavalry breaking through. He believed that bullets had "little stopping power against a horse."

The most stupendous artillery barrage yet in history was to begin the assault: over seven full days, 1,437 British guns rained a million and a half shells on the enemy along an 18-mile front. Five gigantic mines were dug under the German trenches. Enough equipment to supply a considerable city, including 120 miles of water mains, was concentrated behind the British lines. Fourteen British divisions, some 150,000 men, had been brought up, along with five French divisions, to oppose the six German divisions known to be dug in at the Somme.

It was to accommodate the French artillery observers, in fact, that the generals set the attack for 7:30 A.M., in the full light of morning and not at first dawn when, as experience had shown, a man often could get clear up to the enemy lines before being spotted. This time, the high command said, it would not be necessary to run. After that terrible bombardment, there would be no living creature left to fight and no barbed wire entanglements worth mentioning.

"You will be able to go over the top with a walking-stick," one brigadier told his men. "When you go over the top," another said, "you can slope arms, light up your pipes and cigarettes and march all the way to Pozières before meeting any live Germans."

Doubtless the order forbidding the men to run need not have been given, for each soldier carried a minimum of sixty-six pounds, some as much as eighty pounds. There were his pack, his rifle, bayonet, 220 rounds of rifle bullets and two grenades. There were the two gas masks, the spade, the wire cutters, the empty sandbags. There were, for some, carrier pigeons in crates, two glass wine bottles full of water, and on the back of the pack, shiny triangles of tin to help rear observers spot them. Normally, attackers would sprint for enemy trenches the instant a barrage lifted, trying to catch the defenders before they could struggle up out of their dugouts and mount their machine guns. But not on this day.

The mines went up at 7:28 A.M., and two minutes later, in the stunned silence that followed, British whistles blew like a thousand doormen summoning a thousand cabs, and 66,000 British soldiers scrambled out of the trenches, formed their lines, one man to every three paces, and began the march at a prescribed ceremonial step of one yard per second toward the German lines—anywhere from 50 to 700 yards away. Cheering was not allowed. No one was to stop for the wounded or so much as look to right or left. The Tyneside Scottish marched to pipers. The Eighth East Surreys came out kicking footballs.

One German witness, an army surgeon, estimated that 14,000 British died in the first ten minutes.

It seems that the German dugouts, thirty feet deep and deeper, had not all been destroyed. The British generals had not investigated this possibility. During lulls in the bombardment the week before, British raiding parties had found many enemy trenches fully manned and the thickets of wire before them virtually undamaged, though cluttered about with dud shells. This information had been passed back to headquarters but had been rejected on the grounds that it was impossible.

At one-minute intervals now, more waves of infantry came on, plodding across the churned ground. The handful who reached the enemy wire ran back and forth searching for openings; German machine guns concentrated on those openings. Though in some cases so many men were killed trying to get out of their own trenches that their bodies impeded traffic, the troop move-up was handled quite efficiently. By the end of the day nearly 120,000 men had been thrown into the advance.

In that one day the British casualties, dead, wounded and missing, came to 57,470, or half the attacking force. That is about two casualties per yard of front. One division lost three-fourths of its infantrymen, 6,380 soldiers. In an army which during the entire first year of the war was not allowed steel helmets, officers were expected to mark themselves out with Sam Browne belts and swagger sticks: three out of four officers in the attack were casualties.

July 1, 1916, the first day of the Somme, was the bloodiest day in British history. To find comparisons by which to judge this single day's losses by one army, it is necessary to add up the casualties of entire wars. For example, Britain lost more men on July first than it did in the Crimean, Boer and Korean wars combined.

The Germans lost about 8,000 men that day.

More than enough has been written about Haig—who after July first decided that he had not intended a big breakthrough after all—about General Sir Henry Rawlinson who had insisted on the slow march, the daylight attack and the rigid plan for a rolling barrage during the advance, a barrage that pelted the German rear all day, uncoordinated with the floundering infantry. Many bitter words have been written about the indecisiveness and obstinacy behind the so-called diversion at Gommecourt and about the men who fought their way across to the German lines on that hot morning only to mill around without leaders and finally to drift back for lack of a plan. The role of dud shells, estimated as high as one-third the total, and the infantry training that clung to Boer war concepts because the top officers never visited the front lines (Haig considered it his duty not to view wounded men, for the sight upset him and he feared it might affect his judgment): it has all been told before. In the end, one is reduced to reciting numbers.

The Somme offensive plodded on for 140 days. The cost to the British has been listed as low as 415,000 men and as high as 481,842. One reason for the divergence of figures is that 73,412 men simply vanished, which makes record-keeping difficult. Allied losses altogether have been set at 794,000, to the Central Powers' 538,888. The British gains over the four and a half months amounted to a strip of No Man's Land averaging about five miles in width along an eighteen-mile front. Most of that ground was recaptured by the Germans in one day during their 1918 offensive.

From Haig's dispatch of December 23, 1916: "There is sufficient evidence to place it beyond doubt that the enemies' losses in men and material (on the Somme) have been very considerably higher than those of the Allies."

Tom Easton—private, Second Battalion, Tyneside Scottish, 1914–1919—was standing in his driveway when I finally found his place, a retired miner's cottage near Choppington, fifteen miles north of Newcastle. He was in shirtsleeves, though the September afternoon had turned raw, and a wind that smelled of coal dust was twirling the few white hairs still on top of his head. Stocky, not more than 5 feet 4 inches, with ruddy, firm skin, he looked far younger than his seventy-nine years. And he was smiling.

This was a surprise. Historian Martin Middlebrook, who had given me Easton's name, had warned that north country people were apt to be standoffish: "If you're not going to get along with a Geordie, he'll let you know quick enough." Also, there was the accent, famous even among Britons for its guttural impenetrability.

"But Easton's the man to talk to about the first day on the Somme," Middlebrook had assured me. "Easton was one of the ones who got to the other side and came back."

Fascinated and horrified by the story of the Somme, I

vaguely planned to find some survivors. Maybe I could take one survivor, I thought, and build an article around him. So here I was in Choppington.

The house was of red brick with a motto on the front, "After Toil Is Over." A birdhouse stood on a pole in the middle of the walled front yard where healthy roses and daffodils stood in the casual precision that marks the work of a gifted gardener. From this house the long row of bungalows stretched down the street, each with its tiny yard, each with curtained windows facing another row of cottages across the high-cambered pavement. At the near end of the road stood a general store and a pub and a tobacconist's; at the other end, over a slight rise, I could see more rows of spare little houses, some empty flatlands and the gray sea.

In my search for the place I had driven all the way to Newbiggin, a seaside hamlet flanked by more bleak marshes and smelling not of salt but of coal dust. Ever since the Roman invasion, coal had been dug up here. The Romans discovered sea coal, or coal exposed by erosion along the seacoast, and as early as 1236 it is recorded that the monks of Newminster Abbey in Morpeth obtained permission to break up sea coal on the shore by Choppington. In 1635 there was "a coal pit" at Bedlington, and in 1693 the first mining lease was granted to a local citizen. Before the mines there were weaving and nail making in Bedlington, Cambois and "Slikeburn," mentioned as settlements as far back as 900 in the Boldon Book, an early chronicle.

Easton took me around to the back door, facing onto a paved alley. The inevitable tool shed stood there at the head of his second garden, this one in vegetables, and close to it was a handsome fence Easton had made from discarded schoolroom furniture.

Just before he opened the door he pointed across the flats to a distant green hillock with sheep grazing on it. It was the tip of the mine where he had worked fifty-two years, often 250 feet down.

"I worked twice that deep in Germany," he said quietly, "when I was a prisoner. There's nothing built over that land because it's honeycombed, you know. They left the pithead buildings, you can see them there, they have a little factory there now. That big black one there—" a snort of irritation—"they told us that wouldn't be visible from here. When I was on the County Council. And we believed 'em. Look at it."

He was seventeen years a councilman for Northumberland County and still served on an advisory group as honorary alderman, he told me. In the midget kitchen he picked up a superb potato that he had just dug from his garden. "See that," he said, more or less to himself, "Common Market wants 'em banned. For rust. A potato like that. . . . Vegetables? I've got flowers and vegetables front and back. I'm feeding half the county."

The tiny vestibule opened into the front room, where a card table was set up with two places at it. Mrs. Easton, as I was always to know her, rose with some effort from the sofa, gave me a shy but sharp glance from behind her glasses and murmured that I would be wanting some lunch. I denied it. Didn't want to put them to any trouble, I said. Had had a late breakfast. But they seemed to know all about the schedule of my train from London and furthermore had correctly guessed that I had been too absorbed in renting a car, learning the left-handed British highways and finding this modest row of bungalows in an entire landscape of modest bungalows to have managed lunch.

Protesting mildly, I sat down to a platter of chops,

boiled potatoes, cauliflower and bread while Easton, across from me, nibbled at some lettuce and tomato slices. Before I was aware of it, Mrs. Easton had covered the table with plates of sausage rolls, toasted teacake, cheese, cucumbers, tomatoes, fruitcake and three different pies she had made, along with, of course, the tea itself. She retired to her sofa and her knitting. She ate nothing, having recently suffered thrombosis, Easton explained.

"I bet you haven't eaten in a long time," she said. And a few minutes later, as I flagged somewhat: "Come on, boys, have some more strawberry pie. You're not eating."

The little room, snug rather than crowded, seemed to be full of clocks; there were seven of them on the mantel, on the piano, on walnut-and-glass cabinets of fancy china. Easton's son William was a clockmaker in Newcastle, I learned. ("It's a gift, honey," Mrs. Easton said, "and mind, he's left-handed.") On the mantel were a photo of a granddaughter, a golliwog, a plaque with the insignia of the Tyneside Scottish. While Mrs. Easton put away the tea cozy, rolled up the blanketlike table cover, folded the tablecloth and put them all away in a cupboard, Easton began rummaging in the piano seat, which he called his office.

"We're a bit tight for space here," he muttered. There were more papers in an old suitcase behind the armchair, and the unused front vestibule was stacked with papers. "You should have seen it when I was in politics." He put his hand up to shoulder height, ducked his head and grinned.

When he retired in 1961 he got the cottage free from the government, he said, and the television too. A good deal, he said.

"Good deal," murmured Mrs. Easton, watching out the

front window for the paper to arrive. "And you workin'
fifty-two years in the pits."

It wasn't easy, moving in from the larger place where
they had raised four children. "She start a-bubble," he
smiled, nodding at his wife. "But it's still near the family
here."

Some of the best memorabilia were still in the hands of
a local historian. ("Impatient, he was. Would ask a question and then say I wasn't answering it. Some of these
things you can't answer in a few words.") His approach
to my cautious first questions was methodical: the reply
would come in the form of an anecdote, perhaps ten minutes long, and any interruption would be handled sum-
marily as a footnote. "To finish my story . . ." he would
continue firmly, and there was nothing to do but ride out
the anecdote. I found it usually answered my original
question quite thoroughly.

Gradually we worked into the war, how he enlisted at
the age of eighteen, one year under the minimum, late in
1914, and how the recruiting officer told him to go around
the block and come back when he was a year older, and
how his brother Joe, who actually was nineteen at the
time, had to lie too to make it come out right.

"He died last year. We were together through most of
it. He won the Military Medal, but he wouldn't tell you
about it."

Nimbly rising from the straight-back chair, Easton
darted into the bedroom next door to find the "TS" armband ("you can imagine the names we gave it") which
was all the men were issued at first by way of uniform.
Though the four battalions officially became the Twenty-
first through Twenty-fourth Northumberland Fusiliers,
part of the amazing volunteer civilian army that General

Kitchener conjured up to augment the battered professional Old Contemptibles, the survivors still call themselves the Tyneside Scottish.

All I could glimpse of the bedroom was the foot of a bed, a bookshelf and a bureau crammed in together, almost touching. Still, it was bigger than Tom Easton's first bedroom.

He was just six months old, the third of six children of William Easton, a mine foreman, when the family moved into a house provided by the West Sleekburn colliery: one large room downstairs, one room upstairs reached by a stepladder near the fireplace. "We had quite a happy childhood," he said.

From *Coalmining*, A.R. Griffin: "The houses of these pit villages were built in rows. They were small insanitary structures. In Scotland many of them were single-roomed hovels, with roughly built walls about five feet high, bare earth floors and no foundations. Some of these were still occupied in the 1860s and probably later. In Durham and Northumberland standards were a little higher. There were some one-roomed cottages there, too, but most had either one or two ground floor rooms and a loft. . . . Many of the houses were still occupied in the 1930s; indeed, quite a lot survived into the 1950s. . . .

"In many cases the water had to be drawn from standpipes, of which there were one or two for each row of (80 or more) houses. Slops were still carried away down an open drain at the backs of the houses. Earth closets (privies) were now provided in wooden or brick structures in the yards of the houses, but these were shared and many people preferred still to use them as little as possible."

(Though the earth closets were emptied about once a month by "the midden man," usually a neighbor, these houses had to be kept closed all summer because of the flies that swarmed around the privies, which often were barely eight yards away.)

"In Northumberland and Durham the men were engaged under yearly bonds until the 1840s and this tied them to their employers although not nearly so strongly as serfdom. . . . In some parts of Durham and Northumberland, it was traditional to have a stewpot, replenished daily, always on the hob. The only other downstairs room (besides the kitchen) was the pantry, usually built under the stairs. The two bedrooms would measure somewhere between 10 feet and 12 feet square as a rule and at least one of them would have a fireplace.

"An essential part of equipment for all these houses was the zinc bath which was usually kept hanging on a nail outside the back of the house. On bath night the bath was put on the hearth rug and filled with hot water from the boiler. One lot of water, topped up as it grew cool, did for the whole family. Some miners took a hot bath in this way every day, but many contented themselves at most with a strip-wash at the kitchen sink or in a large bowl."

"West Sleekburn village has been my base from 1897 to 1961," Easton said. "Now, this lies in the urban district of Bedlingtonshire—which is an honor for such a small council to call themselves a shire. We also have East Sleekburn village a mile away and then Sleekburn village. Choppington is another colliery village."

The move in 1961 took him half a mile up the road to the hamlet of Stakeford, served by the Choppington post office but still in the church parish of Cambois. It would be many conversations before I learned to sort out all these places.

He drew a map showing West Sleekburn: two rows of houses with gardens back to back and more gardens flanking the colliery waste area; the great rectangle of the colliery with its shaft, stables, shops, reservoir and railway siding; a third row of houses between the tip and the tracks, and fitted here and there compactly, the school and schoolmaster's house, two Methodist churches, the Church of England's St. Peter's, the co-op store, the Institute and the pub.

"It was always a pit village, starting out from 1860. We moved coal for one hundred years. The Bedlington Coal Company worked five collieries here till Nationalization, that was in 1947, and the colliery agent always lived at Bedlington."

The afternoon was waning. I hadn't learned a great deal, though I hadn't expected to on this first day. I needed to reorganize my questions. I wanted to know more about the career in politics, of which I had been given no inkling. I had to sort out the war anecdotes, for Easton's unit fought in almost every major action on the Western front, from the Somme to Arras to Passchendaele, and he himself was captured early in 1918, so had much to tell about working in German mines as a prisoner.

He was delving into his box of mementoes again: old photos of officers ("Look at those men, those faces. A man would follow 'em. Calm and straightforward, you could trust 'em."), invitations to banquets, ceremonies, memorial services, a picture of the five Maitland brothers ("two killed on the First, one killed later, two wounded"), postcards of the church at Albert on the Somme, the square

14

at Arras called Suicide Corner, a faded photo of himself and other Somme veterans on their 1962 trip to the battlefield. He had returned there many times, made friends with farmer families who still used the heavy, long-spiked World War I barbed wire on their fences.

Easton, whose school education stopped when he went into the mines at thirteen, taught himself French during the war. ("I was put in a dubious position because I could talk to the madams," he muttered.) His accent, like mine, was serviceable if not elegant. Just as I was leaving he told me the address of his son William. I wrote down "George Street," which was what I thought I had heard. Peering over my shoulder, he shook his head.

"George Street," he repeated, with the half-swallowed Geordie "r."

"George Street?" I said.

He waved his hands impatiently. Two or three times before, we had had trouble with his northern speech and my American drawl, but this was the worst yet. I was baffled. We glared at each other in frustration.

At last he held up a finger, his eyes alight. "Eglise!"

"Ah," I said. "Church Street!"

We laughed. We had found a common language.

From Tom Easton's diary: *I left school in the summer holidays of 1909, when I got my "Labour Certificate," which was a form that enabled us to leave school having been educated sufficiently to satisfy the authorities, but I was not pressing to go to the Pit, so I ran about until October, helping my mother, hoping to go to be a tradesman of some sort.*

I was an asset at home. Even to look to my older brother Robert (an epileptic) took a great deal of worry from my mother. He was a keen fisher, so off we used to go to the River Wansbeck near to the Sea or along the River Blyth on the north side, walk both ways and stay all day. This was also a source of worry to me, for he used to sit with his legs dangling over the jetty, and should he have taken a fit, well he would plunge into 12 feet of water, but it never happened. . . .

Then I was caught up one day by the colliery undermanager, a very respected man in the village. He said, "What do you think you are doing, not at school?" and I said, "No, I left school in July."

He was astounded. "Running around doing nothing," he said. "Get yourself up to the colliery office tonight at 5:30. I want to see you." So I got home, not too happy, and told Mother what Mr. Millar had said.

"Well, you will have to go and see what he wants. . . ." For in those days, if you refused, pressure could be put on with your parents' accommodation in colliery-owned property. So I duly got licked up and presented myself at the colliery office at the top of North Row which also was the residence of the undermanager and the pay office. I was called in by Mr. Millar, who always had us take our caps off when we entered.

"So you are running about doing nothing, eh? Well, you have had a long enough holiday now, so get down home and get to bed early, for you start on the Pit Heap tomorrow morning at 6:30 and report to John Wood the weighman who will fix you up."

So I withdrew saying "Yes Sir" and making no protest, and off down home to give the news to Mother who was in a dilemma on what I would wear to work, for this was very dusty and dirty work, standing over coal tipples and taking the tokens off the tubs or calling in the numbers to the weighman as each tub was weighed. What I looked like the next morning when I arrived on that Pit Bank I can never imagine, but I was greeted with much laughter by all there. Someone else's cap, too big for me and down on my ears, an old jacket of my father's hurriedly cut down for me but still no fit, boots belonging to my elder brother.

We had to go home again from 8 A.M. to 8:30 for breakfast, then at noon for an hour to get our midday meal, then carry on till Pit finish, *in all about 10 hours a day, and we were paid 10d (about 20 cents at the time) and only paid each fortnight. There was no pay on the Friday for me as we were paid in a running-on system, so on the next fortnight I was paid the marvelous sum of 1 and 8 (about 40 cents) less deductions which were 3d each week to the Colliery Institute, where we read all our papers and comics, played billiards and dominoes. So I landed home with 1 and 2 for my first pay in the Coal Mining industry for 20 hours' work.*

Tom was late for our next appointment, so I talked briefly with his wife Edith, who was seventy-four and like her husband from a mining family. She told me about their son and the three daughters, the eldest of whom was forty-nine, and the four grandchildren and two great-grandchildren. They all lived within a few miles of Choppington, and one daughter visited them every week to take advantage of ladies night at the nearby baths. I was to hear much more about the problems of bathing, of keeping miners and their clothes clean with only the simplest of facilities.

Mrs. Easton said her son William was the first in four generations of Eastons to break away from the mines. Tom and his father worked in the pits for a total of 113 years.

Family memory stopped with Tom's grandfather, Robert Easton, who died in his seventies in 1915. ("Grandfather came from the border country, I think," Tom said once. "My granny said she was part Irish. We used to have a metronome on the piano—I gave it to my uncle Robert because he had the name—and the plaque on it said, 'Presented to Mr. Robert Easton, the bandmaster of the Guidepost Brass Band.' Beyond that, I don't know. He was a miner, oh yes, he was a shaft sinker. Once he was

17

sent to Germany to study some of the new techniques of the time.")

When Tom did show up, he appeared somewhat abashed. There was a bandage on his forehead. He had been moving some lumber at the county center where he regularly helped give aged and housebound people a day out, and a board had fallen on him. I offered him a ride to the clinic up the street, where he could have the cut treated. He accepted immediately, though on the way he confided that it was his first visit to any sort of hospital in many years.

On the way home he reported the receptionist had asked him for his medical card and he had told her, "In the archives," meaning in the piano stool.

"She said come back tomorrow, but I told her don't be givin' me any answer like that, I'm here on emergency."

Mrs. Easton, who had taken the whole incident with a couple shakes of the head and some clucking, added, "He'll put it into his diary, he'll say I went to Blyth and got me head bonked."

Both of them tended to speak in asides to me, and frequently Tom (and later Mrs. Easton too) would touch me gently on the shoulder or knee to emphasize a point.

We settled down to another sprawling tea, with plates of homemade currant jam, teacakes, toast, pies, sausage rolls, shortbread, mincemeat tarts and fruitcake covering every inch of the tablecloth, while Tom rambled about his enlistment in 1914.

"We thought it would be over by Christmas. Everyone did. It was going to be a summer camp, you know. For awhile we went on in the pits as before, but the summer waned and the colliery was down to a three-day week and the three wage earners in the family were down to half-pay, so my brother and I put things together and decided to enlist."

Tom wanted to be a sailor, but he couldn't afford the ride to Newcastle, the nearest navy enlistment station, so he and Joe and some friends walked the four miles to Blyth to join the army. It was November.

The disorganization was epic. A friendly if blustering rivalry between the area's Irish and Scottish residents sent men pouring into the recruiting offices around Newcastle to join the twin brigades, Tyneside Scottish and Tyneside Irish, each with four battalions of about one thousand men apiece. Answering Kitchener's call and the jingoism that now swept Britain, men from all walks of life volunteered, some managing to stick together with their friends and thus form the so-called "Pals" units, close-knit groups of office workers, professional people, miners, factory workers. Signing up in their hundreds and thousands, the volunteers discovered that the government wasn't ready for them, nor were the private citizens who had put up money to raise troops in the venerable British tradition. Soldiers were billeted everywhere, anywhere. When the Easton boys arrived by train at Newcastle they were assigned to a large rooming house along with two hundred others. They were not the first; the place was packed already.

"There were queues all day," Tom said. "Queues for all three meals. You had to go up five flights, winding around and around, moving up step by step until you got your breakfast. Queues to go to the toilet. To wash up."

Men slept on the stairs, to be trampled on by casual passers-by in the night. Men lay nose to toes on every level space available. One spent the night on the piano.

The only semblance of uniform was the TS armband and a blue-and-white shoulder cord.

"Every day was better, though. We got shuffled into companies and we were drilled. Have to run four miles and then walk some more to queue up for breakfast. Then more drills. The uniform came on day by day. One day we'd get a glengarry, then a pair of boots. We thought we were to have kilts, but that didn't happen. They did let us cut our pants short in summer." (Much later the Tynesiders, still not allowed to wear kilts, were awarded a small patch of dull "sandbag tartan" to wear on their caps in recognition of the unit's bravery. One Geordie studied the little square and muttered, "Man, there won't be any left to wear it if we have to earn it this way.")

"We thought we were soldiers already, and we'd march along on the cobblestones of Newcastle and feel pretty good, but we weren't disciplined. Our NCOs were our own people. One night we were sleeping in a church, and we had a tenor, a lad with a fine voice, and someone said, 'Give us a song,' so he went up into the pulpit and sang and we all lay back there on the floor with our hands behind our heads and listened. And then the sergeant came in and said to stop this bloody nonsense. But some private turned to him and said, 'Aw, let him finish, mon.' "

Scene on Newcastle drill field: Officer walks past sentry, who fails to salute. Officer: "Don't you know who I am?"

Sentry: "No, I don't know who ye are."

"Well I am Captain Smith."

Sentry (putting out his hand): "Well I'm pleased to meet you, I am Private Jones and you'll have a grand time here among this mob."

From Tom's diary: *After church parade on a Sunday we were free until Monday morning, so Joe and I walked home to West Sleekburn so that we could have a good Sunday dinner and a rest in bed, and we had to be back at Bedlington Station at 6 A.M. to get the train. What our parents felt about all this, well they never let us know but it must have been a heartache for them. But we lived up to our home and kept to the Straight line. Our older brother Bob took this badly, for he must have missed us very sorely, only girls left at home with the exception of Edwin, just over 8 years of age.*

Eventually the Tynesiders—now officially the Northumberland Fusiliers—moved to the moors outside the Duke of Northumberland's Alnwick Castle, where they built a camp for four thousand men (everything was on stilts, for the Duke had given orders that the grass was not to be disturbed), and here they drilled until the summer of 1915, when they were marched to the Yorkshire coast for their first concentrated rifle practice. Then on to Salisbury Plain for still more drill.

"We had our hair taken off," Tom said, "so we all looked like Yul Brynners. We miner lads had our hair cut short anyway, it was too hard to wash it every day; I have my father's clippers still, in fact. There were a lot of us enlisted from the mines. We never disregarded our parents, no liquor or cigarettes—we weren't bad lads."

"Oooh, you were ruffians," Mrs. Easton put in.

(Tom was a teetotaler, all right, but I'm not so sure about the cigarettes: there is a dim photo of him in uniform with a butt dangling from his mouth. And once he told me how as boys he and his friends would steal the clay pipes left outside the mine by miners going to work, would smoke up the remaining dottle in them and return them before quitting time.)

One night at the camp a drunk tried to get into his bell tent, where sixteen men slept tightly wedged together, feet toward the center.

"He poked his head in and kept tryin' to climb in over everyone, and he was wakin' us all up. So someone took a tent mallet and tapped him on the forehead, and he backed out. Next day he had two black eyes and couldn't understand where he got 'em. Oh, there were some bad boys there."

As Tom finished the story his head ducked into his shoulders, his brows went up and he pressed his finger under his nose, grinning like an elf.

The men were issued Enfield rifles dating from the Boer War.

"We learned to fire sixty cartridges per minute. One lad's rifle went off when we were all standin' there about him. The sergeant roared at him, 'What's going on?' 'Oh it's all right,' he said, 'it can't hurt anyone. My sights are set at zero'."

About this time the specialist units were organized, and the two brothers signed to become signalers, learning flag signals, hand signals, heliograph, Morse code and, every day, marching for hours on end through the pleasant moors and meadows. (Captain to sergeant: "Who is that man up there?" Sergeant: "That is a scarecrow, sir." Captain: "Never mind who he is, fall the man in. . . .")

That summer, newly vaccinated and full of rumors about being shipped to the Dardanelles, the Tynesiders joined some twenty thousand troops of Kitchener's new army in a grand review at Newcastle before "King George V and Lord Kitchener himself," as the diary put it. "Khaki clad men as far as the eye could see on the moor that day, infantry, artillery, cavalry, cyclists, and we were there in position for hours before the great moment came . . . and

22

the King and Kitchener did walk up and down those ranks, for I well remember, when we were given the order Present Arms the butt of one man's rifle left the stock so he presented arms with one piece just held on top of the other until they got past. The wisecrack of the company said to his next hand man, 'What do ye think of him, Geordie?' 'Why mon, he's just like Kitchener's pocket hingin' out'—the King being about five-feet-one and Kitchener six-feet-two. 'Like a little kipper,' he said."

It was a beautiful summer. The Dardanelles move was forgotten, though a few pith helmets were indeed issued. The men considered themselves hardened soldiers now, and time stopped for long afternoons spent gorging on wild strawberries along the moor roads or trapping rabbits in miners' expertly made snares, the game to be stewed in wash basins on the round stoves at the center of each hut. A marquee had been set up for the occasional concert or comic monologue by patriotic music hall celebrities, and of course football and cricket teams materialized wherever the men went.

Townspeople near the various camps were friendly, for a soldier was still a novelty in those days, and Tom met several girls who invited him into their homes to meet their families.

"One in particular wrote to me throughout the whole of the war," he recalled in a letter, "until I was taken prisoner of war, when correspondence was so limited we had to address it to our families, and this girl thought I had gone the way of all flesh and perhaps forgot about me. After getting back home I wrote to her in Alnwick, and the response was instantaneous, letters followed, a rendezvous was arranged—no buses in those days—she arranged to sit by a certain gate on the Warkworth-Alnmouth road on a Sunday afternoon. . . . I was up at 5

23

A.M. and away to work at 6 A.M., worked my shift, home, washed, had my dinner, got my father's push bike ready, set out on not too good roads in those days, did my 14 miles and sure enough my little girl friend was there. What a meeting we had, although there was nothing deep or sexual between us. We were great friends and had been separated four years. We walked back to Alnmouth, some three miles, where I took her to tea, and all the tales I had to tell. She informed me that she was engaged to another chap in Lancashire, so we were free and aboveboard; she lingered on till she lost her train to Alnwick which was over five miles away, so we walked all the way back to her home town nearing 10 P.M., and after parting I had to cycle back to my village 20-odd miles away. But to meet her again it was all worth it. Such pure friendship was rarely found."

At last the unit was ordered to France, to be precise on January 10, 1916, as Tom effortlessly recalled. "We were put in reserve behind the front at first. More training. The first day, we were pretty excited. One lad went out to take the brass nosecap off a German shell for a souvenir, and a stray bullet got him in the backside. I think the shock alone almost killed him. We didn't do any more hunting for nosecaps."

Soon there were short spells of actual trench life in what was then a quiet sector of the front at Armentières: four days on the line, four days off. By spring the Tyne-siders were ready for special training: rehearsing for the Big Push. They learned to advance under a creeping barrage and practiced attacking trenches on terrain that resembled the Somme area.

"When they needed trenches dug, they got the miners to work on 'em. Had to be 7 feet deep, 3 1/2 wide at the top, 2 1/2 at the base, and each man to dig one yard. One lad dug halfway down and quit. When they asked him he said, 'Well what's the next lad going to do?' Thinkin' in terms of shifts, he was. Pit lads, they were."

All through those days at Armentières there was what the dispatches referred to as "wastage." "Of course," Tom wrote, "our men were being lost all the time, stray shells got parties of men working, machine guns found a target, snipers got their man and occasional raids were organized upon the German lines to keep up the aggressive spirit of the men and boost morale. But seldom did they go off without someone being killed.

"Men's faces and hands were blacked and after careful preparation from the Brigade staff downwards they would leave our trenches and crawl in the darkness to the German barbed wire. The cutting party would cut a gap in the wire. Now this had to be carefully guarded by one or two men as this was the only means of getting back after the raid. Bombers would advance with hand grenades and move towards where the sentry was, bombs would be thrown and the men would jump into the trenches and grab any German they could lay their hands upon, and having got these out of the trenches would create as much havoc as possible. At a signal by the officer in charge they would retire through the wire. These raids always created a storm, for the Germans would contact their artillery and shelling would go on for hours from either side."

On exhibit at the Imperial War Museum in London (housed in what was once Bedlam asylum) is an entire caseful of prehistoric weapons. It is only upon reading the labels that one realizes these things were used during World War I. For the first two years British soldiers were trained and equipped for the wrong war, a war that existed only in the imaginations of the staff officers. They even dressed for the wrong war, with their Indian puttees. Rapid-fire work with the rifle was stressed, but once on the line the men found that they used their rifles little if at all. To show a hair of one's head above the trench meant instant death—for the first time in human history it was not an advantage to be tall—so there was no question of leaning out there on one's elbows ripping off round after round. In this war something very different was needed for killing.

One sees in the museum: dozens of clubs bristling with nails or boot studs. A stiff spring with a heavy bolt for a head. A sawed-off gun barrel wrapped in leather. A steel gauntlet with punch-dagger jutting out in front. An officer's cane loaded with lead. A shillelagh. A whittled "godendag" exactly, the label reads, like the clubs used by the Flemings at the battle of Courtrai in 1302. Both sides used medieval mantraps to discourage raiding parties. Both sides experimented with the crossbow for hurling grenades, and early in the war some British units actually were issued a version of the Roman catapult.

From Captain Reginald Leetham's diary in the Imperial War Museum library: A raid on a German trench. "Our men were armed with knobkerries also and they smashed a few German skulls in. Murray, an officer in our company, caught a great big Hun about a foot taller than himself a knockout blow with his fists, and then trampled his face in with his feet. . . . Then they found a great big underground dugout and threw a dozen bombs in. The yells and groans were awful to begin with but all was silent after six bombs had been thrown in. . . . They brought back five wounded Huns as prisoners for our staff to get information from, but halfway across four of them turned sullen and stupid and refused to walk further so our men left their bodies where they shot them. . . ."

Conditions in the trenches have been described by many survivors: the incredible mud, into which horses and men sometimes sank clear out of sight, the stench of excrement and rotted flesh and explosives and gas, the maggots that writhed underfoot and oozed up from cracks in the dried mud, the rats, gorged on human meat (they preferred eyes and livers), some of them as big as terriers and as bold as cats, the churned-up battlefields lost and won and lost again a dozen times since 1914, in which the earth itself seemed to be composed of dead bodies, where arms and legs and heads would protrude from the trench walls and had to be covered with sandbags pinned up by cartridges or chopped off with a shovel and buried. The eyeballs on the duckboards. Hardly any of this appears in the Easton diaries. They are concerned more with the business of getting through the day.

"When you occupied the trenches," he wrote, "nothing was done about shaving, button cleaning or even washing . . . but when Haig assumed command (December, 1915) these orders were all revoked. Buttons were cleaned, boots dubbined, one had to be shaved, and generally soldiers became very much smarter. Steel hats had to be worn always on duty, cooking began in the trenches, places were constructed in which a cook could do the company's food, and this made for a much more cheerful soldier also. Tea was brewed, bacon fried and other meals made, provided that battle conditions allowed. It meant that big army dixies had to be carried from the support line to the front line, and this was done by a rota so that all did the chores."

In some units, he told me, the large metal dixies were carried coolie style, one slung on a pole between two men. But it was common to see a soldier from the mining districts—strengthened by a lifetime of hauling his family's water cans from the village standpipe—lugging two dixies by himself, one in each hand.

"Rations were brought up at dusk by the transport lines to the end of the communication trench, and each company had its own party out from the trenches to receive its rations in sandbags and often we were loaded up with two bags slung over each shoulder, plus your rifle which you were never without. . . . The rum rations were brought in with the stores and this was served out to every soldier each morning.

"For myself I did not take this ration at any time, but I used to go and draw it, and the soldier pal who wanted it used to follow immediately behind me. As the sergeant gave the ration from the dugout door it was passed back, he drank it and I returned the Oxo tin which was usually the measure, a large tablespoonful.

"As the years passed, things began to be built from boredom. A shovel and sandbags were always on hand, and we built shelters for our own comfort and for those who should follow in. . . . In the north from the Aubers Ridge to nearly the Belgian border we could not dig a foot downwards, for this filled with water, so we had to build barricades."

Late in June, as the gigantic and hugely publicized buildup for the Big Push reached a climax, Tom was assigned to Battalion headquarters as signaler, together with his brother. The suspense began to make everyone slightly jumpy, though the main feeling reported by many survivors was excitement over being in on what they believed would be the kill. Even the fact that the German positions all along the twenty-mile line looked down upon the British, so that enemy observers could watch the new trenches being dug, the new units being marched in, the telephone lines strung and, all the way to the horizon, supplies being stacked for the attack, failed to dull the exuberance of thousands of young Britons who had been promised a cakewalk for their first major experience of combat.

"The bombardment opened on 24 June, for the infantry attack was still planned for the 29th, and the gunners settled down to a daily routine. Each morning they fired a concentrated barrage for 80 minutes, using every available gun. This was to be cut to 65 minutes on the morning of the attack so that the infantry could go over with the Germans still expecting another 15 minutes' barrage. For the remainder of the day a continuous, but steadier, barrage was fired. At night half of the guns rested but the barrage was supplemented by heavy machine guns, which put down specially harassing fire on the enemy's rear, hoping to cut off the garrisons in the trenches from supplies and relief. . . . The task of cutting the barbed wire had been given to the 18-pounders but nearly all the ammunition they were using was shrapnel shells."

The First Day on the Somme, **Martin Middlebrook**

"How did our planners imagine that Tommies, having survived all other hazards . . . would get through the German wire? Had they studied the black density of it through their powerful binoculars? Who told them that artillery fire would pound such wire to pieces, making it possible to get through? Any Tommy could have told them that shellfire lifts wire up and drops it down, often in a worse tangle than before."

With a Machine-Gun to Cambrai, George Coppard

In their bunkers thirty feet below the surface, the Germans waited. Some went insane. Throughout the bombardment men took turns on watch, to report the instant a barrage stopped. Great emphasis was laid on getting men and machine guns into place within seconds of the final shell explosion.

Georges Blond, in *Verdun, 1916,* tells of enduring a typical World War I bombardment which "lashed and ripped the earth, tossing huge chunks of it up into the cloud of smoke, dust and debris which had replaced the breathable air. A rain of branches, stone, fragments of metal, cloth and human bodies fell uninterruptedly from the yellowish sky. No other movement was possible; the human presence was reduced to flattened terror. In every man not yet smashed to bits the violence of the shock produced a constriction of the blood vessels that wiped out every feeling but sheer animal fear and the desire to hide underground the palpitation that still persisted in the center of his body, just above the diaphragm. Men's eyes were not closed but wide open, their pupils dilated: they did not blink when, a few yards away or even within reach, the bodies of their fellows were transformed into a flat spot beside them or torn to pieces or erased from their sight."

When the attack was held up for forty-eight hours because of heavy rains, Easton's signaling section remained where it was, in the advance headquarters dugout.

"Although cramped we could lie down when off duty. All were to be in the trenches every morning at stand-to half an hour before and after dawn. Everyone naturally was very tense but did not care to show it. We went about our duties as usual, right up to stand-to that morning of the First. Then we had to collect our equipment and make our way to the rendezvous point, the third line trenches, which had all been previously marked out. No one in the mood for letter writing, for all letters had to be censored and company commanders had more important things to do. . . ."

Official postcard issued to British troops in the line: "Nothing is to be written on this side except the date and signature of the sender. Sentences not required may be erased. If anything else is added, the postcard will be destroyed.

"I am quite well.

"I have been admitted to hospital sick/wounded and am going on well/and hope to be discharged soon.

"I am being sent down to the base.

"I have received your letter/telegram/parcel dated_____.

"Letter follows at first opportunity.

"I have received no letter from you lately/for a long time.

"Note: Postage must be prepaid. . . ."

"What we had to carry: A signaler carried a flag, a signaling disc used from trench to trench, a field telephone, reel of wire, your rifle, twice the ordinary ammunition, 60 rounds in the pouches, 60 rounds around the shoulders in bandoliers, pack, haversack, trenching tool and either a pick or a shovel, plus water bottle full and two additional glass bottles of water on top of the pack wrapped in a sandbag. We could hardly climb out of the trenches.

"While being pent up we never felt fear, we had been so drilled to expect little or no resistance. A forward observation officer from the artillery kept our staff entertained by explaining the different shell bursts by the color of the smoke."

Tom settled back, hands clasped before him, face tranquil. "I still remember that morning," he said. "A beautiful summer morning, though we'd had a bit of rain earlier. The skylarks were just singing away; it makes you wonder at the marvels of nature, to be able to adapt to this. Then the grand mine went up, it shook the earth for nearly a minute, and we had to wait for the fallout. The whistles blew and we stepped off one yard apart, going straight forward. We were under orders not to stop or look or help the wounded. Carry on if you're fit, it was."

The Tyneside Scottish front was 50 yards from the German lines, but the men had been brought back to rear trenches because of the bombardment, making the distance to be covered 150 to 200 yards.

A signal sergeant whom Tom had admired lost his nerve at the moment of climbing from the trench, and the men had to push him up into the open. Almost immediately, he suffered a coveted "Blighty" wound that would take him home to England.

"So then I went into the German trenches," Tom added casually. "It was all over by eight-thirty. The Germans were shocked too. My own division's guns weren't supporting us but were moving up the valley, making

crossfire on Mash Valley. I wasn't tired or afraid or anything. . . ."

He talked on, and I didn't stop him, but I really had
expected more than this. The crucial minutes of the
charge had come and gone so fast I had all but missed
them. It was going to be a matter of bringing him back to
that morning, that hour, again and again until he could
remember it in detail.

From the diary: *Then Zero hour came, and the Great Mine was
exploded at 7:28 A.M., shaking the very earth on which we stood,
and throwing into the air thousands of tons of earth. When this had
settled, the whistles blew and we clambered into the open and began
our advance, keeping in line and extended order. Men began to fall one
by one. One officer said we were O.K., all the machine-guns were firing
over our heads. This was so until we passed our own front line and
started to cross No Man's Land. Then trench machine-guns began the
slaughter from the La Boisselle salient. Men fell on every side, scream-
ing with the severity of their wounds. Those who were unwounded dare
not attend to them, we must press on regardless. Hundreds lay on the
German barbed wire which was not all destroyed, and their bodies
formed a bridge for others to pass over and into the German front line.*

*Bombers carried out their duties and pressed on up the communica-
tion trenches, also passed along and secured the flanks. There were few
Germans, mainly in machine-gun posts. These were bombed out, and
there was fewer still of us, but we consolidated the lines we had taken
by preparing firing positions on the rear of the trenches gained, and
fighting went on all morning and gradually died down, as men and
munitions on both sides became exhausted.*

Tom unfolded an old trench map, almost worn through at
the creases. The first, second and third stages of the pro-

jected advance were marked on it in crayon.

"When we got to the German trench we'd lost all our officers. They were all dead, there was no question of wounded. About twenty-five of us made it there."

Eventually, by way of a small saphead that had been blown close to the German line, supplies and a telephone cable were brought up. Establishing a base in a German dugout, the signalers managed to contact advanced Brigade headquarters. Tom showed a pencilled message he had transmitted that day, asking for Very lights since the daylight was fading.

"I found wounded lying about," he said, "and had to drag 'em to the dugout. There was one officer on hand by this time, and I had people lying about outside and I was only a kid."

By evening some thirty severely wounded officers and men were collected from barbed wire and shell holes and brought to the dugout. There was no question of moving them back to the British lines before dark, and anyway there were no stretcher bearers left alive. Many wounded died during the long day.

"Bob Wear was hit. He kept saying, 'Can't you get me a glass of water?' The water bottles were all broken, of course. As you know, bleeding dehydrates you. I asked the major: 'Can I have some water for Sergeant Wear? He's crying out for water.' The major said I could give him some of mine, which was a dispensation from the rule that you weren't supposed to share your water."

Tom snorted, gazing at the old map.

The diary: *We did not stay long in possession of our signal station, for the Royal Engineer Signals from Brigade HQ came through the sap and took over from us, stating that this point was to become Advanced*

Brigade HQ for the further pushes that were to take place on the days following.

And so the day wore on, no rest, no letup. Wounded men pleaded for water, but water was at a premium, for the day had been hot. Having found my signaling officer dead just short of the German trenches, I took his personal belongings to hand in at Battalion HQ and dusk slowly fell.

Bob Wear had been attended by me most of the day, and I got permission to get him over to our own lines. So four of us got him on a groundsheet and dragged him back over No Man's Land into our front line, and we did not escape being shelled and fired at. Bob pleaded for us to leave him. Why waste your Bloody lives for me, I am half Bloody dead anyway. But we persevered and got him over, hunted up a stretcher whose team had been killed and made our way down to Becourt Chateau, delivered our charge and the papers that I carried, got drinks of tea and made our way back and reported to the officer in charge. We never rested all night, and dawn came again, everyone tense and built up for a German counterattack which never came on our front. . . .

I was called by the officer commanding troops of the 19th Butterfly division to signal with my flags troops in our old front lines. As I did so, the lines of troops rose up and came over in extended order. They passed us and away on to the present front line, and as the last company came over he thanked me and went on with his battalion into battle. We held the back areas until they had consolidated their positions, and during the night we were withdrawn and put in brigade reserve just in front of the Usna-Tara ridge. There we lingered for the day, given something to eat and nearly slept on our feet; this was our third day without rest. Then the remnants of a once good battalion was marched away to Millencourt to rest. Only one officer survived the day without being either killed or wounded.

Pleasing to note my brother Joe also survived this bloody day, so at least we had something to be thankful for.

Lieutenant Kenneth Macardle, Manchester Regiment, Ninetieth Brigade, at Montauban, described in his diary —now at the War Museum—a chill white mist early on the morning of the First, followed by bright sun that turned the white-yellow shrapnel smoke balls pink in the sky. At 8:30 A.M. his unit went through two other brigades which had attacked in the first wave.

"A shell would burst and a tidy little section in the file would crumple up and be gone. . . . I caught a glimpse of young Wain, his face haggard with pain, one leg soaked with blood, smoking a cigarette and pushing himself forward with a stick. His voice was full of sobs and tears of pain and rage. 'Get up, you __, Blast your souls, get up!' I waved to him and he smiled and dropped—he knew it was not absolutely up to him any longer."

Macardle was killed July 9 on the Somme.

Edward G. D. Liveing, a subaltern with the County of London Regiment, started the day in a brick-floored communication trench about three miles behind the front. He reported being awake most of the night in the crowded trench, whose walls were overhung with dewy grass and flowers. The wind blew east, with a few fleecy clouds. "There was the freshness and splendour of a summer morning over everything."

During the final barrage he became restless to get moving. He also noted that "the idea of an afterlife seemed ridiculous in the presence of such frightful destructive force." He went out at last at 7:32 A.M., with the third wave.

"Just in front the ground was pitted by innumerable shell holes. More holes opened suddenly every now and then. Here and there a few bodies lay about. Farther away, before our front line and in No Man's Land, lay more. In the smoke one could distinguish the second line advancing. One man after another fell down in a seemingly natural manner, and the wave melted away. In the background, where ran the remains of the German lines and wire, there was a mass of smoke, the red of the shrapnel bursting amid it. As I advanced I felt as if I was in a dream, but I had all my wits about me. We had been told to walk. Our boys, however, rushed forward with splendid impetuosity. . . .

"A hare jumped up and rushed towards and past me through the dry, yellowish grass, its eyes bulging with fear. . . . At one time we seemed to be advancing in little groups. I was at the head of one for a moment or two, only to realize shortly afterwards that I was alone. I came up to the German wire. Here one could hear men shouting to one another and the wounded groaning above the explosions of shells and bombs and the rattle of machine-guns. I found myself with an officer of C Company, afterwards killed while charging a machine gun in the open. We looked around to see what our fourth line was doing. My company's fourth line had no leader. . . . I turned around and advanced to a gap in the German wire. There was a pile of our wounded here on the German parapet.

"Suddenly I cursed. I had been scalded in the left hip. A shell, I thought, had blown up in a waterlogged crump hole and sprayed me with boiling water. Letting go of my rifle, I dropped forward full length on the ground. My hip began to smart unpleasantly, and I felt a curious warmth stealing down my left leg. I thought it was the boiling water that had scalded me. Certainly my breeches looked as if they were saturated with water. I did not know they were saturated with blood."

World War I rule of thumb: In the first forty-eight hours of a major battle, 20 percent of the troops involved would be wounded, on the average. The estimate comes from John Laffin's *Surgeons in the Field,* which also notes that the most terrible feature of this war was the multiple wounds inflicted: "A man might have chest, head, spine and abdomen wounds; the same shell fragment might traverse the abdomen and the chest and these abdominal-chest wounds formed a dangerous and difficult class to deal with."

Laffin cites three classes of wounds: rifle or machine-gun bullet, shrapnel or pieces of shell (some of these were so massive they took two men to lift them), bomb or grenade. Shell wounds were the most common in the trenches, and the worst, "for the jagged fragments made large holes, splintered bones, lacerated tissues and often carried with them fragments of germ-laden cloth or equipment." Field surgeons saw few bayonet or bludgeon wounds because most of those were immediately fatal.

Because the war was fought on rich farmland, "practically all wounds were infected from the outset, through the skin, clothing, missiles or soil; many of the wounded lay in the open for hours or days before aid could be rendered and were suffering from shock, exhaustion and loss of blood."

"The horrors of the first-aid post were standard—men holding their intestines in both hands, broken bones tearing the flesh, arteries spurting blood, maimed hands, empty eye sockets, pierced chests, skin hanging down in tatters from the burned face, missing lower jaws . . . men with chunks of steel in their lungs and bowels vomiting great gobs of blood, men with legs and arms torn from their trunks, men without noses and their brains throbbing through open scalps, men without faces. . . ."

The Realities of War, **Philip Gibbs**

From Captain Leetham's diary: "We arrived at these dugouts at 11 P.M. (June 29). They were about six feet wide and ten feet long and ten men had to sleep in each of these. Young, Price, Murray and myself, the four officers chosen to lead D Company in the battle, had one to ourselves, and very uncomfortable it was too, as we had only one servant who was not going into action to take back what we could not carry into battle."

July First: "When one got within 500 yards of the front line one began to be rushed by panic-stricken wounded fellows running to get their wounds dressed. . . . I got to my position and looked over the top. The first thing I saw in the space of a tennis court in front of me was the bodies of 100 dead or severely wounded men lying there in our own wire. . . . I sent my runner 200 yards on my right to get into touch with our right Company, who should have been close beside me. He came back and reported he could find nothing of them. It subsequently transpired that they never reached the front line as their communication trenches had caught it so much worse than mine, and the communication trench was so full of dead and dying, that they could not get over them. . . . Those three battalions who went over were practically annihilated. Every man went to his death or got wounded without flinching. Yet, in this War, nothing will be heard about it, the papers have glowing accounts of a great British success. . . . 60 officers went out, lots of whom I knew. I believe two got back without being wounded.

"I must tell you now that we never went over; our order

to attack was canceled at 5:30 in the afternoon. . . . The dead were stretched out on one side (of the trench) one on top of the other six high. . . . To do one's duty one was continually climbing over corpses in every position. . . . Of the hundreds of corpses I saw, I only saw one pretty one—a handsome boy called Schnyder of the Berkshires who lay on our firestep shot through his heart. There he lay with a sandbag over his face. I uncovered it as I knew he was an officer. I wish his Mother could have seen him —one of the few whose faces had not been mutilated."

"The 2nd Middlesex came back with 22 men out of 600. . . ."

Haig, April 14, 1915, minutes to the War Council: "The machine-gun is a much overrated weapon and two per battalion is more than sufficient."

"For the British, who had staked so much on 1 July, the meager achievements were a bitter disappointment. In simple terms, the right wing of their main attack had been successful; the center and left had failed. At Gommecourt, the attack had not eliminated the salient even if the diversionary function had been fulfilled.

"Territorially, the lower arm of the huge letter L of the front line had been moved approximately one mile farther north, but the new front line here faced north towards the rest of the German lines rather than eastwards towards their rear.

"The attack had taken three of the German fortified villages: Montauban, Mametz and Fricourt—the last being evacuated during the night following the battle— out of the thirteen which were in the day's objectives, plus certain trenches, dugouts and redoubts that had taken much labor to build. At no point had the German main second line been breached. . . .

"Eighty-four battalions had attacked in the first hour, a total of some 66,000 men. Roughly one-third, by hard fighting, skill and some luck, had gained all their objectives. Another had nothing to show for their losses, except small and vulnerable footholds in the German trenches. The final third had been completely repulsed; not a living attacker was inside the German wire, unless as a prisoner of the enemy. Five out of the nine villages due to be taken during the day should have been captured in the first hour. Not one had fallen."

The First Day on the Somme, Martin Middlebrook

From Haig's dispatch of December 23, 1916: "The first phase opened with the attack of First July, the success of which evidently came as a surprise to the enemy and caused considerable confusion and disorganization in his ranks. . . . In view of the general situation at the end of the first day's operations, I decided that the best course was to press forward on a front extending from our junction with the French to a point halfway between La Boisselle and Contalmaison and to limit the offensive on our left for the present to a slow and methodical advance. . . ."

From *The Times History of the War,* **Vol. IX, published in 1916:** "Passing rapidly over the ground which separated them from their opponents, our men carried the enemy's front line trenches with an irresistible rush which the dazed and demoralized occupants were quite incapable of withstanding. . . . By the end of July 1 we had made considerable progress. The right of our attack had captured German trenches on a front of seven miles and to a depth of 1,000 yards, besides taking several strongly fortified villages. In the center of our attack we gained ground over a front of four miles, capturing many strong points; but up to the evening the enemy still held out at many others, and the struggle continued to be very severe. North of the Ancre Valley we were much less successful, and German counterattacks even compelled us to yield a portion of the ground we captured. . . .

"The result of the first day's fighting was, upon the whole, very satisfactory for both the British and the French. It was not a lightning-like stroke, intended to pierce the German lines right through, but rather a continuous and methodical push to make sure of the ground which had been devastated by artillery fire. This involved less loss of life and more certain results."

"The German report on the first day's fighting was curious and somewhat amusing," *The Times* commented, because of its conclusion that the British attack had not succeeded.

It was still light when we finished. Both of us were talked out, and Tom had an evening meeting of his county welfare committee ahead of him. He walked me to my car, we agreed to meet the next afternoon for a final session and, slightly anxious about finding my way in the gathering gloom, I started out, map on the seat beside me. That morning I had driven twenty-five miles up the Tyne valley to Corbridge and had reserved a room at a tiny inn, apparently the last room available in the entire township, for this was the center of an ancient Roman establishment and stood only a short drive from the best section of Hadrian's Wall plus other attractions: a Roman camp, baths and a temple of Mithras.

A chill night had fallen by the time I reached my inn, and I settled down to a dinner of steak and pigeon pie ("a traditional Northumbrian recipe," the menu insisted), a drink before the fire and a review of my notes and questions for the next day before turning in. The room, like the one the night before in Morpeth, was closet-sized, with a small window overlooking a back alley, and equipped with a wash stand, bureau and one chair. But the narrow bed was deeply comfortable, and I never doubted that I would need every bit of the two-inch layer of blankets.

The people at the bar seemed undismayed by my Americanness, and I found none of the edgy silences so common to many east London pubs in the presence of foreigners. One talked about dogs, for there was always a dog lying by the hearth, and at breakfast (a massive slice of bacon, two eggs, fried tomatoes, mushrooms, toast and jam) one talked about the weather. It looked like rain, everyone agreed.

On the green shoulder of land that was Corstopitum, a major Roman army station, it looked like rain at the very least: sullen, vast gray clouds rushed past, close overhead, and the winter-smelling wind pressed coats against bodies and sent hats flying. Strolling among the ruins of Roman dormitories and granaries, now mostly mere rows of stone molars sticking up from the grass, I tried to imagine how a Roman soldier must have felt, stationed in this wild country, surrounded by these short, sturdy, fur-clad northern people. It must have been an unloved assignment.

High on the ridges to the west, shrouded in towering

oaks, stood a series of grand houses, neo-Georgian mansions, classic Victorian country houses with tall Gothic bay windows and many chimneys, built by the mine owners. "Oh, they're not the real thing," the guard told me. "They're copies. Can't be more than 150 years old."

Later in the morning, as I trudged up a long trail to Hadrian's Wall, a lashing rain swept the hills, turning the path to slick mud and making the neatly dressed stones of the wall glisten. From the parapet of this great rocky fist raised in defiance of an implacable enemy, I could see for miles: a sprawling valley covered by the long rough northern grass so reminiscent of the rugged coats of Angus cattle or Shetland ponies. A green world, deep, rich green. The trunks of the windswept trees were green, the fence posts were green, the stones themselves were green, covered with a fine patina that seemed to have been blasted into their surface by wind and time.

In the rain I hurried back to Choppington, by now easily familiar with the twistings and turnings of the road. Once again the tea things were spread out on the card table. Once again Mrs. Easton lay on the sofa knitting and listening. Tom had found a group picture of some signalers, taken just before leaving for France: "Dead . . . dead . . . wounded . . ." the stubby finger passed along the line of young uniformed figures, "leg off . . . missing . . . made it . . . killed in the pits . . . dead. . . ."

Supposedly, we were talking about Tom's experiences during the rest of the war, a kaleidoscopic period of waiting and marching and fighting and waiting again, great chunks of empty time glittering with bright moments of fear or hilarity.

"A man would be on sentry duty at dawn standing on the firestep," he recalled, "and some guy would go by below and pull his leg—literally—and say, 'You heard the news?' Sentry would glance down. 'What bloody news?' Guy would say, 'Lord Robertson passed a quiet night.' " He chuckled to himself. "It saved you. Things like that."

A portrait of an officer, carefully saved, reminded him of an incident on the march away from the front after July first. The officer had told the men cheerfully that things weren't so bad, that after all, there'd be plenty of rum for them now.

"The lads sat down on the spot. Wouldn't go a step further. He was a time gettin' us up again."

He paused and then said, in his curiously formal way, "We were always taught to respect our betters. But with confrontation with those betters during the war years, we came to see that we were much the superior beings in many fields."

Once a young officer, just out of Edinburgh University, stood watching Tom and another man digging a cable trench on the eve of the Somme attack.

"We dug and chatted, and the officer listened. The other guy was a lance corporal. A miner. He was with the County Durham Brass Band. Well, we were havin' an argument. 'You pitmen blow yourselves up a bit,' I was sayin'. I said they rewrote the scripts to suit their own range, while we in the orchestra interpreted the script of the composer, not the band conductor's whims. Well, he denied all this, and so I said, 'Right-o, you play to me the last Triumphal March from Tannhauser.' He could do it with just his lips and his hand, didn't need a trumpet. And I said, 'See, you played two minims to the bar. You're leavin' out the demisemiquavers.'

"So then the officer broke in. He says, 'I thought you people were pitmen.' Corporal says, 'So we are. What do you think we are, pigs that live in a pig sty and eat grass and just lie around?'

45

" 'No,' says the officer, 'I never want you to even dream that I do. But I was totally unaware that you were people with culture and intelligence. That quite surprises me, and I apologize.' "

Tom shook his head reflectively. "The ignorance of the educated. . . ." He grunted. "Ten days later I took his papers from his body when he was killed, and on the way back to headquarters I had a look at his record book. He kept records on all the men. Naturally, I looked up my own name. It said, 'He can be trusted in any emergency.' "

Quietly, he added, "That's a code to live by. That's all you need to say about a man."

Did he ever kill?

"I don't know of deliberately shooting any Germans. As signalers we were the sheltered elite, that's what they used to tell us. We always carried a gun, though. I went on one bombing raid with about twenty men; the signalers stayed behind (that is, in No Man's Land) with the wire. Another time I got the officer to call off a raid because it was streaming moonlight."

At Passchendaele the terrain was so muddy that luminous tape was laid down to direct men to the trenches. At Poelcapelle, not even a trench system was left, after the endless shelling and the rain.

"We were relieved after forty-eight hours at Poelcapelle. We were sitting in a reversed German pillbox, which wasn't much use backwards in terms of defense. We were in the mud up to our knees, and we had a stretcher over our heads to keep the rain off a bit. The ration parties had all got lost, and about the only thing we had was rum. Plenty of rum, there.

"Our group got ready to go back, and the officer said, 'Well Easton, you're the leader. You're the only sober man in the lot.' So we went zigzagging along the duckboards.

The guys fell off a lot. And when high-velocity shells started coming down we hit the mud on either side. Oh yes, the water was polluted. . . ."

"Falling into even a shallow hole was often revolting, for the water was foul with decaying equipment, excrement, and perhaps something dead, or its surface might be covered with old, sour mustard gas. It was not uncommon for a man to vomit when being extricated from something like this."

In Flanders Fields, **Leon Wolff**

"That same time," Tom said, "two men got drunk and went off, and I tried to find 'em before they got themselves courtmartialed. I went around asking people, 'Seen a couple of Scotties layin' around here?' But nobody had. Eventually I found them in a shell hole. They were leaping about and claiming that they were galloping horses. One of them got the DSM [Distinguished Service Medal] later."

Did he take any liquor at all during the war? Perhaps the ritual tot given the men just before going over the top?

"Oh no, I abstained. Mine was the greater tribulation, because all that was done in a clear mind. There were days of abandonment. . . ."

He had seen his share of death and horror but was never plagued by nightmares. It seemed easier for him to talk about it than about his own feelings.

"You remember them as they were. One particularly, a beautiful lad, at Arras. He was the first I seed lying face up. There was a tiny hole in his heart. He was the same type person I am, avoided all extravagances, wouldn't say boo to a cat. There was another. Musical, he was. Found a mouth organ once in a German trench, and he'd give us a tune on it. There was a group of them all gathered around, and a shell came right in the middle of them. He had no face on, but I knew it was Billy by the cowlick of his hair."

Billy lies beneath the plains of Arras, he added, where the Tynesiders spearheaded the offensive in 1917.

"I got to say this, I was a good clean-livin' lad. It often came to me to be what we termed the hut orderly. One day a woman came to the hut seeking Ned Mason, that was her husband. This was in our training days. 'He's away on weekend pass,' I said, 'with his wife.' 'But I'm his wife,' she says, 'and he never comes home. Where can he be?' I told her the address in Newcastle where I knew he'd be. She went there.

"He comes in Monday morning, face as long as a fiddle. 'Somebody's been spillin' the beans,' he says. 'Well, you don't have to look any further,' I said. He was not so big as I but it wouldn't have mattered if he had been. I said, 'I did it, I told her, what you gonna do about it, and you with three bairns and a wife at home.' I heard no more about it."

As he spoke, his face tightened, his mouth drew thin.

"In the raid of June '16 I fell over someone lying in the trench. 'Ned, is that you?' 'Yes, I'm done for, would you sit me up.' He was struck vertically by a shell fragment, his whole abdomen was out. I pushed him together and buttoned his tunic and sat him up. His next words were—" (his voice thickening, Tom pressed the bridge of his nose between thumb and forefinger) "—'By God, what I would have given to live a life like you.' 'You can still,' I said. 'There's time, make your peace, man.' He died in my arms.

"Another guy, I found him sitting on the firing step when he was supposed to be going up. Had his back to the wall, and I thought he needed encouraging. I said, 'You're not going up?' 'No,' he says, 'I thought I'd just sit here awhile and rest a bit.' Well, I was worried that he might get arrested, put on charge. Then the guy said, 'Can you hear the band playing?' 'No.' 'Can't you hear it?' He held his arms out. 'There's my old father,' he says, 'they're waitin' for me.' And he fell forward, and I saw he had no back. These things shake you."

From the diary: *The only time I was on charge in my army career —after the Somme I had developed an awful rash down the front of my thighs, also on the lower part of the abdomen, and we had shortened trousers cut off just above the knees in summer time. Well, after about three days' marching this was like raw meat, with the heat and the rubbing, and on this day I could not stick it any longer, so I told my sergeant I was going to fall out, never thinking about getting a chit, just sat by the side of the road until the last of the battalion passed and the whipping-in officer came to me and asked for my chit.*

I said, I have no chit. What, no chit? Well you will be on a charge as soon as we get to billets. Get in the ambulance there. A horse-drawn Red Cross cart.

Sure enough, after we got our meal, the sergeant major came on. You have to report at the orderly room, get dressed up. So with the sergeant major and two escorts, in I was marched to the barn that was the orderly room. What's the charge, sergeant major? Falling out without permission Sir. Hmmm, very good.

He was new to the battalion, this officer, but he said, I have looked at your record, and you have not got one mark against you. What is the meaning of falling out without permission? I said, This was an oversight, Sir, for I could easily have had permission from Sergt. Hartley, but I felt I was justified in doing what I did. He said, And how do you feel justified, and I said, Would you care to see my reason for falling out on the march? He said, I'm sure I would. Very good Sir. So I undid my belt and dropped down my pants and pulled up my shirt. He exclaimed, Good God, you have never marched four days in that condition. I'm afraid I have. Sergt. Major, dismiss this man. Get him out. But he must report to the medical officer. . . .

After examination the MO said, You should be in hospital, but I had no desire to leave my unit after all that we had been through together, and I told him so. Very well, he said, we shall give you treatment. And this treatment was given to the orderly: he took the top off each pimple with a scalpel, and after that I was washed down with a liquid. It was awful. Next day back again and through the same process, but the next day I went and as Jack started his job I said, I am having no more of this treatment, you're making me worse. Jack gave me a wink and told me to get out.

The Sergt said that we had orders to move into the trenches and he wanted an advance party, so I said to put my name down, and away I went to the trenches again at Vimy Ridge. . . . I made my way along the trenches and called at the first aid post. There was Dr. Henry, an old colliery doctor from County Durham. I showed him my condition and he questioned me. I felt that we had drunk all kinds of dirty water in the Battle of the Somme and this was the result. Had I been to the Dardanelles? No. Had I been with any women? NO NEVER. Come here every morning and I will soon put you right, and we were in there 18 days, and at the end of the period I was as clean as a new born baby.

When we got back to billets I was ordered to report sick, so I went along to see the MO. How are you now? Fine Sir, would you care to have a look at me? Oh yes. So down came my pants and he nearly had a fit. Who has managed this? MO in the trenches, Sir. What did he do? I think you better ask Dr. Henry, Sir. Can I go now? Yes, get out, damn you.

From *Surgeons in the Field:* "New and dangerous complaints were trench foot and trench fever. Trench foot was caused through men having to remain for long periods knee deep in water until the feet turned into a mass of chilblains. Sometimes gangrene set in. . . . Sentries slipped under the mud in their exhausted sleep and their bodies would be dug out next day. The food was sodden, and the men kept themselves alive on rum, the officers on whisky." Trench fever, similar to influenza or typhoid, was traced to the louse. Another new experience for doctors was gas. Nine months after the war began gas was introduced, first chlorine gas, then phosgene, then mustard gas. "Mustard gas was an evil thing, blistering the skin and, in some cases, stripping a man's entire body of skin." Smelling only faintly of garlic or mustard, it often wasn't detected until the body and especially the eyes had been covered by the oily substance. It was so pervasive that a man could carry a bit of it into a dugout on his boots and could affect everyone in the place. The case of an Australian soldier was cited, Trooper Rolph, who lived for five years in a bath of warm water after losing all his skin.

"We were all pepped up for the big German invasion in March 1918," Tom recalled. "We were to bear the brunt, they told us. I drew listening post for March 21, and the invasion was to start on the 19th, so I said I'm in the clear, I'll either be dead or it'll be over by then. . . ."

The diary: *One of our duties was to provide a signaler and telephone each morning before dawn to go out with the listening post, who crept over No Man's Land to a point in front of the German wire and took* cover in shell holes. So for this we drew lots, and I drew 21 March. Well, I said, that is OK for me, for Jerry was going to kick off on the 19th according to the last prisoner taken, but the 19th passed and the 20th, so in late afternoon I told the corporal that I was going out to the front line to be sure of my way in the darkness of the next morning so that I could make my rendezvous. Getting kitted up, telephone with cable, etc., I made my way to the rendezvous. All gas masks at the alert position, we made our way out through our own wire and crossed to the German wire, and all was dark and quiet.

Just before dawn hell was let loose on our right and left, terrific bombardment was laid down, and worse when our own gunners took up the challenge. Lights and flashes of every hue filled the sky, but on our immediate front nothing much had fallen.

Then the officer in charge suspected that gas was being employed on this sector, and I was requested to let Battalion HQ know, but on trying to make contact I could get nothing, and I told the officer. He swore a bit, but I offered to take the message to the rear. I collected my kit and scrambled back to our trenches and made my way to my brother's Company HQ to get the message down. It appeared that the advanced Battalion HQ was on the line, but no reply from Battalion HQ in the sunken road.

As the day wore on, shelling began about the trenches we had occupied, and we learned that Battalion HQ personnel had all been taken prisoner and many killed, even advanced Brigade HQ were taken prisoner, and we were still in the front line. The Germans had come up from behind.

We were surrounded by Germans, and as darkness fell we moved out into the open, down the hill by the side of a disused quarry, stopping, moving forward as quietly as possible towards where our troops now lay. And sure enough we were challenged by English soldiers and back into the line now formed. Capt. A.W. Mark was decorated for this achievement. . . . In the morning, which came all too soon for us, we held on against odds for a good while, our Lewis guns doing excellent work in the open, but many were wiped out, and in the late morning we were to fall back off the crest toward Boiry, where we consolidated in some trenches that had been hastily dug, and that evening we were relieved by the Guards. Battle casualties for this action were 3,179 in the division. After tea and something to eat we were marching again to the Le Cauroy area. . . .

Home Leave: *On June 18th (1917) while lying in reserve we were visited by Sir Harry Lauder and he even sang a song or two for us, one was, Keep Right On to the End of the Road, he having lost two sons was out here visiting their resting place. . . . On to July 1st, anniversary of our debut as a fighting unit, and a dinner was arranged for the "Old Boys," and only 150 of the Battalion responded to the original roll call serving today, from about 1,000 men. Only one year, 850 had gone either dead or wounded.*

On August 25th the Gold Ring given me by my Mother on leaving for service broke, it was worn to nothing on the inside of my hand, so I put it away safely until I saw her again. On Sept. 13th I started out on Home Leave, left for Le Havre and arrived there at 4 P.M., sailed at 9 P.M. to Southampton, then up to London. Left London at 2 P.M., arrived Newcastle soon after 7 P.M., we could only get a train to Blyth so did the other 4–5 miles on foot.

Just took things easy, and out most days to picture halls, dance halls, etc., until the morning of 25th September, at 7:30 walked to Bedlington Station. We always left quietly and our parents did not accompany us to the trains. Got to Waterloo Station about 5 P.M. and were allowed to spend the night at the Union Jack Club. Slight enemy raid that night and there were a few casualties. Put aboard the HMS Antrim and left at 9 P.M., entered Le Havre at 4 A.M. but did not disembark until 7 and climbed aboard a train that duly got us to Peronne at 10 P.M. and joined the battalion who were out on rest.

A touch of home: Huntley & Palmer, perhaps the world's most famous purveyors of elegant tinned biscuits, supplied biscuits for the fighters. These were not elegant. They were khaki brown, four inches square, and looked grimly nutritious. Other great British names in luxury foods helped feed the troops. Keiller's sent marmalade in the traditional stone jars, and Oxford's sent cans of "parchment-coated suet puddings."

Officers were permitted to outfit themselves, and Robert Graves gives this list of supplies he bought for his return to the front after recovering from a wound: "a pocket-torch with a 14-day battery and a pair of insulated wire-cutters strong enough to cut German wire (the ordinary army issue would cut only British wire), a pack like the ones carried by the men but lighter and waterproof, an eiderdown sleeping bag in an oiled-silk cover. I also took a Shakespeare and a Bible, both printed on India paper, a Catullus and a Lucretius in Latin, and two light-weight folding canvas armchairs, one as a present for the quartermaster, the other for myself."

From an Easton letter: "In all my service abroad, we only had two home leaves, and there was a certain amount of loneliness apart from your own family. Leave was a short matter to us, about six days at home. We had to travel so far north and there was no allowance for this, it was 10 days from unit to unit. One reason for this loneliness was that the majority of our generation was at war. Those who were left, well we did not see fit to mix with them who it could be felt were shirking their responsibilities, but we went to dance halls, cinemas and other entertainments and I noticed little deference. The girls were keen upon their own boy friends but always friendly to us. We always led a good life and our family was always with us. We came on leave together, so we had each other's company. I used to go out for a long walk in the daytime down to the seashore and I met one of the old village Standards when coming up the road. He said, Is that Tom? and I said, Yes it is. Why lad, he said, they have made a man of you all right. Now, his son had never attempted to join HM services, so I said, You have never got your Bill out for a man to be made of him. So he went dumb and said nothing. Other than that I never recall any coolness towards us, but naturally we had been away two years on a military mission and we could not expect to fit in.

"The other angle was, people were loath to question a soldier, where he had been or what he was doing or even where he was going, and not many questions were asked. My grandmother was alive when I came from France the first time, so Mother said, You want to go over and see Granny Jackson, so off I went in uniform, and she had not seen much of me over the years, but I stayed quite a while and we chatted and chatted, so when I was ready to come away she said, Now Honey, when ye gan back, if them Germans start thrawing them guns at ye, get yoursel back hame as soon as ye can.

"Right-o Granny, I said. When they do start throwing the guns at us it will be time to pack in."

Robert Graves, in _Goodbye to All That:_ "England looked strange to us returned soldiers. We could not understand the war-madness that ran wild everywhere, looking for a pseudo-military outlet. The civilians talked a foreign language; and it was newspaper language. I found serious conversation with my parents all but impossible. Quotations from a single typical document

55

of this time will be enough to show what we were facing":

A MOTHER'S ANSWER TO
"A COMMON SOLDIER"
By *A Little Mother*

A Message to the Pacifists . . . A Message to the Bereaved . . . A Message to the Trenches.

To the Editor of the *Morning Post*

"Sir—As a mother of an only child—a son who was early and eager to do his duty—may I be permitted to reply to Tommy Atkins, whose letter appeared in your issues of the 9th inst.? Perhaps he will kindly convey to his friends in the trenches, not what the Government thinks, not what the Pacifists think, but what the mothers of the British race think of our fighting men. It is a voice which demands to be heard, seeing that we play the most important part in the history of the world, for it is we who 'mother the men' who have to uphold the honour and traditions not only of our Empire but of the whole civilized world.

"To the man who pathetically calls himself 'a common soldier,' may I say that we women, who demand to be heard, will tolerate no such cry as 'Peace! Peace!' where there is no peace. The corn that will wave over land watered by the blood of our brave lads shall testify to the future that their blood was not spilt in vain. We need no marble monuments to remind us. We only need that force of character behind all motives to see this monstrous world tragedy brought to a victorious ending. The blood of the dead and the dying, the blood of the 'common soldier' from his 'slight wounds' will not cry to us in vain. They have all done their share, and we, as women, will do ours without mur-

56

muring and without complaint. Send the Pacifists to us and we shall very soon show them, and show the world, that in our homes at least there shall be no 'sitting at home warm and cosy in the winter, cool and comfy in the summer.' There is only one temperature for the women of the British race, and that is white heat. With those who disgrace their sacred trust of motherhood we have nothing in common. Our ears are not deaf to the cry that is ever ascending from the battlefield from men of flesh and blood whose indomitable courage is borne to us, so to speak, on every blast of the wind. We women pass on the human ammunition of 'only sons' to fill up the gaps, so that when the 'common soldier' looks back before going 'over the top' he may see the women of the British race at his heels, reliable, dependent, uncomplaining.

"The reinforcements of women are, therefore, behind the 'common soldier.' We gentle-nurtured, timid sex did not want the war. It is no pleasure to us to have our homes made desolate and the apple of our eye taken away. We would sooner our lovable, promising, rollicking boy stayed at school. We would have much preferred to have gone on in a light-hearted way with our amusements and our hobbies. But the bugle call came, and we have hung up the tennis racquet, we've fetched our laddie from school, we've put his cap away, and we have glanced lovingly over his last report which said 'Excellent'—we've wrapped them all in a Union Jack and locked them up, to be taken out only after the war to be looked at. A 'common soldier' perhaps did not count on the women, but they have their part to play, and we have risen to our responsibility. We are proud of our men, and they in turn have to be proud of us. If the men fail, Tommy Atkins, the women won't.

"Tommy Atkins to the front,
He has gone to bear the brunt.
Shall stay-at-homes do naught but snivel and but
sigh?
No, while your eyes are filling
We are up and doing, willing
To face the music with you—or to die!

"Women are created for the purpose of giving life, and men to take it. Now we are giving it in a double sense. It's not likely we are going to fail Tommy. We shall not flinch one iota, but when the war is over he must not grudge us, when we hear the bugle call of 'Lights Out,' a brief very brief, space of time to withdraw into our secret chambers and share, with Rachel the Silent, the lonely anguish of a bereft heart, and to look once more on the college cap, before we emerge stronger women to carry on the glorious work our men's memories have handed down to us for now and all eternity. Yours, etc.

"A Little Mother."

From a military training lecture, "The Spirit of the Bayonet," by Colonel Ronald Campbell: "You've got to get down and hook them out with the bayonet; you will enjoy that, I can assure you. . . . The only time that a German can find pluck to kill with the bayonet is when he comes across one of our own wounded; he will plunge the steel into their hearts as they lie unable to defend themselves. When you see this done, can you have any sympathy for them? No! Ten thousand times no! Kill them, every mother's son of them! Remember that your job is to kill them—that is the only way—to exterminate the vile creatures!"

From a German diary of the Somme: "The trenches look terrible, all shot to bits. Numerous bits of equipment belonging to our dead and wounded are lying about. There are a large number of corpses about and we can hardly bear the smell. . . . Frightful artillery fire on the hill to our left, which the English hold. The clouds of smoke rise as high as a church tower. I feel a human pity for the men there, although they are our worst enemies. Hatred of the English is great among us. When we were marching off it was especially impressed upon us that we were to annihilate them. It is said that there was no need for this gang of mercenaries to fight, that it was only money that impelled them. I will not judge them so harshly; perhaps need drove many to lend their aid in this horrible murdering."

In *The Times* of July 1, 1916, there is an announcement offering governmental insurance on aircraft and bombardment risks. A model of Sir Roger Casement (sentenced to death for treason that June 29) is appearing at Madame Tussaud's. Hospitality is offered "to a convalescent officer" by "two ladies with a small country house near London."

"Young flying officer, public school and Cambridge, suffering from overstrain" seeks a companion on a Devonshire farm, preferably another officer in similar condition.

An offer of second-hand officers' uniforms and effects —"remember, we also buy reasonably."

At Aeolian Hall, Benno Moisewitsch is presenting a concert of Schumann and Chopin. Professor Kantorez, the Anglo-Russian singing master, announces a recital with his pupil Tamisa, the Anglo-French soprano. Volunteers for a "Women's Tribute to the Sailors and Soldiers of the Empire" include Mrs. Patrick Campbell, Sir Edward Elgar, Miss Myra Hess, Gerald du Maurier, Miss Ellen Terry. An index lists thirty-three special war appeals and charities, from the Army Horses Fund to relief for submarine victims. Another column lists resort advertisements.

A Mulliner Landaulette on a Cadillac chassis, 20 horsepower, is offered for £300.

The proceedings of the annual meeting of the Marconi Wireless Telegraph Company occupy two full pages. A world cotton shortage is predicted.

One William Hawkins has been convicted of "making statements prejudicial to recruiting discipline and fined £100 with an alternative of three months in prison." A clerk at Smithfield goods depot, he was called "Von Hawkins" by his colleagues because of his pro-German statements and "his manner of wearing his mustache."

Bernard Shaw testifies at the trial of a conscientious objector, a Grenadier Guards private who refused to parade. The accused said he had been put in a straitjacket for twenty hours, given a bread and water diet and, when he went on hunger strike, was force-fed.

Prime Minister Asquith declines to recommend August 4 as a Day of National Penitence and Prayer, as recommended by the Archbishop of Canterbury.

The German flier von Boelke shot down his nineteenth plane June 29 over the Somme, it is reported.

A cinema version of Macbeth, "supervised by D. W. Griffith," is featured, as is a film, "Please Help Emily," with Gladys Cooper. Beatrice Lillie heads a vaudeville revue. Other attractions: "The Bing Boys Are Here," La Petite Nina and Her Motorcycling Seals, "Bric-a-Brac," "A Little Bit of Fluff," "Razzle-Dazzle" and "Peg O' My Heart" with Moya Mannering.

(Many a soldier on leave would remember "The Bing Boys Are Here," showing at the Alhambra Theatre on Leicester Square; it starred George Robey and Violet Loraine, and a high point was their duet, "If you were the only girl in the world, and I were the only boy.")

At Marshall and Snelgrove on Oxford Street, a full-length muskrat fur coat costs 19½ guineas. A five-bedroom house in elegant Regents Park is for lease at £80 a year. A "lady bank clerk" is sought, wages 27 shillings a week.

"I looked in vain for those laughing faces so often featured in the papers at home and remembered wryly the journalists' tales of enthusiastic troops eager to get at the Hun."

The Somme, 1916, **Norman Gladden**

Casualty lists, "as reported by the War Office under various dates," ran daily in *The Times.* Separate lists were run for officers and men, the officers receiving one line per name, the men's names and serial numbers run together. Officers also had separate obituaries on occasion, and paid death notices were printed elsewhere in the paper.

The small type allowed about 40 to 42 names per column-inch.

On July 4, the casualty list came to 10 inches for officers and 28 for men. On the fifth it was 12 and 21 inches respectively, with another 31 inches for Canadian and Australian losses. Officers' lists usually were roughly one-third as long as the men's, though sometimes they ran as high as two-thirds.

The total list on the sixth came to 48 inches. On the

tenth, it was 118 inches. By the seventeenth, it was 154.

On July 24, casualty reports covered an entire page, 167 inches, listing 6,108 names. Separate columns for New Zealand and Australian losses appeared on other pages.

By July 31 the lists totaled ten solid columns. On August 5, the paper printed 5,180 more names. On the seventh, 6,092. On the ninth, 5,013. On the fifteenth, 5,550. On the seventeenth, 7,582, and for the rest of August the lists ranged between 4,600 and 6,100 every day.

War novelties on sale in British shops included an inkwell shaped like a German spiked helmet pierced by a sword; a china model of a Tommy driving a steamroller over the Kaiser; postcards depicting Germans shooting babies, having orgies, using civilians for shields; a tea bell with a helmeted German skull for a handle. After the tank was introduced, its shape turned up as an inkwell, a paper-weight, a penny bank, a jewel box, a cigarette lighter, a pincushion, a whistle, a token for board games, and a sugar holder to go with a teapot in the shape of a howitzer.

From the *Bradford Pioneer,* July 27, 1917: "FINISHED WITH THE WAR; A Soldier's Declaration." (This statement was made to his commanding officer by Second Lieutenant S.L. Sassoon, Military Cross, recommended for D.S.O., Third Battalion Royal Welch Fusiliers, to explain his grounds for refusing to serve further in the army. He enlisted on 3 August 1914, showed distinguished valor in France, was badly wounded and would have been kept on home service if he had stayed in the army.)

"I am making this statement as an act of wilful defiance

of military authority, because I believe that the war is being deliberately prolonged by those who have the power to end it.

"I am a soldier, convinced that I am acting on behalf of soldiers. I believe that this war, upon which I entered as a war of defence and liberation, has now become a war of aggression and conquest. I believe that the purposes for which I and my fellow soldiers entered upon this war should have been so clearly stated as to have made it impossible to change them, and that, had this been done, the objects which actuated us would now be attainable by negotiation.

"I have seen and endured the sufferings of the troops, and I can no longer be a party to prolong these sufferings for ends which I believe to be evil and unjust.

"I am not protesting against the conduct of the war, but against the political errors and insincerities for which the fighting men are being sacrificed.

"On behalf of those who are suffering now I make this protest against the deception which is being practised on them; also I believe that I may help to destroy the callous complacence with which the majority of those at home regard the continuance of agonies which they do not share, and which they have not sufficient imagination to realize."

(Siegfried Sassoon's letter became the subject of angry debate in Parliament. His friend and fellow poet Robert Graves talked to a friend in the Government who "persuaded the War Office not to press the matter as a disciplinary case, but to give Siegfried a medical board.")

From the magazine *John Bull:* "The Huns—vicious in victory, cowards in defeat—deserve no more consideration than a mad dog or a venomous snake . . . to Hell with pacifists . . . We're out for War—let it be War to the death!"

George Coppard: "An enjoyable prank of Snowy's and mine was testing the resistance of the steel helmets that lay scattered about by wielding a pick and bringing it down on one full force. Snowy's forestry-trained biceps were pretty good at it. A good British helmet yielded only a moderate dent, but a dud would burst open down to the shaft of the pick handle. We couldn't very well experiment on our own helmets, in case they should turn out to be duds. Clearly, some cunning contractor had been cheating and a War Office check hadn't been properly carried out."

Wolff: "Saturday night crowds in the City were enormous; in restaurants, night clubs and theaters, earls and seamstresses, welders and landed gentry intermingled with increasing naturalness. Perhaps the pleasures were nervous ones as 1917 waned. . . ."

From *The Times*, August 12, 1916: "Where the injury is to the upper part of the face, resulting in, say, the removal of the nose and one eye, magical results are being achieved in a southwestern district hospital by the provision of masks perfectly counterfeiting the lost section of the physiognomy. Lt. Derwent Wood, A.R.A., is the inventor of the plan. With the help of photographs of what a patient was like before being wounded, he will make a false nose of silvered copper, artistically painted to match the surrounding complexion, which will so far defy detection as to enable the owner to go out into the world again without shrinking, and play his old part in the affairs of men. To do that is to create value for the nation in the truest sense."

Graves: "Patriotism, in the trenches, was too remote a sentiment, and at once rejected as fit only for civilians, or prisoners.... The trench-soldier ... thought of Germany as a nation in arms, a unified nation inspired with the sort of patriotism that he himself despised. He believed most newspaper reports on conditions and sentiments in Germany, though believing little or nothing of what he read about similar conditions and sentiments in England. Yet he never underrated the German as a soldier. Newspaper libels on Fritz's courage and efficiency were resented by all trench-soldiers of experience."

"Trench discipline was stern. 'Field Punishment Number One' was a humiliation. The offender was 'crucified'— tied with arms outstretched to a cartwheel for two hours at a time. Death sentences might be given for desertion or cowardice, although only 346 men actually died in this way."

Battle of the Somme, Christopher Martin

Coppard: "One fine evening, with a big crowd all set for a game, two military policemen appeared with a handcuffed prisoner, and, in full view of the crowd and villagers, tied him to the wheel of a limber, cruciform fashion. The poor devil, a British Tommy, was undergoing Field

Punishment Number One, and this public exposure was a part of the punishment. . . . Troops resented these exhibitions, but they continued until 1917, when the War Minister put a stop to them, following protests in Parliament."

Middlebrook: "Many of the men had been at the Front for up to two years with hardly a break; there was no system of relief for the battle-weary. Those who had been wounded were sent back to the trenches time and time again, and, after each big battle, fewer and fewer of their friends remained. . . . The infantryman's devotion to his immediate comrades and his inborn sense of duty helped to keep him going, but he became very bitter about that part of the army not in the trenches and about all civilians. . . . Self-inflicted wounds, almost unheard of in the early days, became a great problem. Men tried all the old dodges such as chewing cordite or sleeping in wet towels to induce sickness, and being gassed almost became a courtmartial offense."

Nineteen eighteen marching song (sung to "Auld Lang Syne"): "We're here because we're here because we're here because we're here. . . . We're here because we're here because we're here because we're here. . . ."

From the Easton diary: *The weather became cold and clear and keen frosts became the rule, making trench life a really miserable job, but we learned the art of keeping warm, and surviving under these arduous conditions. Socks had to be changed every day and officers had to see all feet rubbed with whale oil daily, and frostbitten feet was put* *among the S.I.W. class, that is, self-inflicted wounds. . . .*

And so we ended another year of almost continuous action. Casualties for the division this year were officers 787, ranks 17,722 (division strength averaged 12,000 at any one time). Northumberland, from which nine of our original battalions came, was not now able to keep up the stream of reinforcements to replenish the great losses of war, for by January 1916 there were twenty-five battalions of the Fighting Fifth overseas.

"When was I taken prisoner?" Tom mused, pouring more tea. "It was April of '18. We were defending a bridge at Nieppe, but we got surrounded. Our people failed to blow another bridge farther along, a pontoon bridge, and the Germans came over on that. So we surrendered." He shrugged. "You do what the officer tells you.

"They made us carry wounded Germans in hammocks or barrows on the way back to the German rear. One guy was carrying a German when he looked hard at him and said, 'This one's dood.' Tipped him out and got a live one. . . ."

The diary: *On April 5th, being informed by the signal sergeant that I was to be left at the transport lines against future emergencies, I felt quite happy, for this was the first time that I had missed anything since coming to France. But by tea time he was back to see me to say, Sorry Tom, but I cannot fill up the stations without you, so take these three men in charge and report to A Company HQ, for we go into the trenches tonight. So that is war, and that night we took over the subsidiary line at Houplines. Things went quietly for a few days, only German spotting planes over now and again.*

Deserters from the Germans said the Portuguese front was to be attacked, so all was done to protect this flank, but we got little time.

On the 7th they began to bombard Armentieres with gas shells from all calibres. This was just behind us, with a quiet wind blowing from the west, but troops in the town suffered severely; the 25th NF in reserve were practically all gassed on the southeast edge of Armentieres, and the cellars in the town were all filled with gas.

After a quiet day and night German guns opened up on the 9th to the south. The volume of sound could only indicate an attack on a considerable scale. All units stood-to, but the Germans broke through the Portuguese line and pushed out vigorously to either flank, and on the afternoon of the 10th we were informed we were to be relieved, so I told my new boys to collect all the bread and cigs lying around and stuff it in their haversacks, but they took no notice. I said it would be a long time before they got another meal except their emergency rations.

At 4:30 we made our way to Houplines and deployed to the left of the bridge as bridge head guard until all troops were safely over. By now it was dark. We had to enter a brewery and hole the vats, and by the time we got out we were over the shoetops in beer, but as we wore puttees in those days it did not affect us much. Some of our good lads said, I never thought I would be over the shoetops in beer and not allowed to have a drink.

The trenches we occupied were knee deep in water, and the bridge was duly blown, but we had to stay to defend from this position, so another miserable night was spent lying with our backs to the trenches but standing on our feet in the water.

During the night the Germans had been getting across the Lys by a wooden bridge left standing farther up, and at dawn on the 11th when the battle opened again they were behind us in Pont Nieppe and beyond. They also were machine-gunning from the nearby houses behind us. The officers decided on the request of the Germans to lay down arms and file out of the position, so after so long a battle over the years, our fighting days were at an end, and my signal boys of the 5th April had passed into captivity after six days of war; my brother Joe being with another company carried on to fight a little longer and as it happened got a military decoration in the later action of this battle by laying out telephone cable under heavy fire.

A letter: "My brother Joe was only 18 months older than I. There was never any rivalry between us, we were great brothers. Joe was dark and strong, which comes from my mother's side of the family, a dependable person at all times. He survived the holocaust also, but he never talked about it, not even after. He got through and was thankful that he did, but never swerved from duty. We had our separate ways but we lived very close and we were always conscious of each other's safety. When I was taken prisoner in 1918 he wrote home and told my mother not to worry about me, they won't kill him, he will turn up, and so I did at Dulmen Camp P.O.W., so he had some faith in my ability.

"When on leave together from France to England it was always Tom who had to find out the trains, the times, the boats. In this respect he relied on me. A grand chap, but never had any children, so he does not carry on the family name. He died at 79 years of age, never complained, just sat on the edge of his bed and died without a word. . . . *God Bless Him.*"

The diary: *We came back to what we called Jesus Farm, now a German dressing station, and stood wondering what next. Our soldier sentry signaled us over and pulling letters out of his pockets made to tear them up, and conveyed to us if there was anything we wished to destroy we had better do it now. I had a belt with German badges and German money that I had collected over the years, and my diary for 1918, so this also went. So off we went with our wounded again*

69

. . . my young friends wished they had the cigarettes that was available to them before we left Houplines. We were handed over to cavalry escorts carrying lances; these people were not so kind as the infantry lads who had just left us. In the late evening we got rid of our wounded, and what a relief, we were sore on the shoulders.

Had to pass the night on the tar-macadam, never been given a bite to eat, and at dawn we were out again on the roads, and eventually we landed in Lille and marched through the town to demoralize the inhabitants. Some tried to help us by throwing bread between the ranks from street corners; any of them who were seen were promptly clubbed with a rifle butt. We were delivered to some old barracks outside town and got a bowl of soup and some black German bread and our first sleep in three days.

April 13th we were given cards to fill in as required by International Law, and these would be posted to England via a neutral country; ersatz coffee in the morning, soup at noon, a little bread and jam. Were paraded through the streets of Lille again to make it appear the whole British army had been taken prisoner. Then we were put into a French fort west of town, Fort MacDonald.

We were confined to one room, about 300 men, but there was army bedsteads in, covered with straw, and we were overrun with lice. We received only one meal a day and not even a drink of water. No washing or shaving, and we just lay on the beds, had a good rest and sang our heads off. Sanitary arrangements were primitive to say the least. Having found a piece of a book, I began again to keep my diary.

On the 24th they called for miners and many of us volunteered, anything was better than this life, so we were moved to other accommodations. . . . At last we were put in wooden rail carriages, traveled all night, the next morning crossed into Germany along the Rhine via Dusseldorf and finally stopped at Haltern and marched some distance up to Dulmen Camp. Next morning we were given a good bath, all our clothes were put into sterilizing chambers, all hair was removed from the body, were medically examined, given clean underclothes, taken to an isolation compound where we had three blankets and a hammock, also were given emergency foodstuffs through the British Red Cross and were really very comfortable.

This was the best accommodation we had had for many years now.

On the 30th we were instructed in regard to any misbehavior, again medically inspected, vaccinated and inoculated, but soup was our only menu, and most of us suffered from dysentery due to this very fact. We got no solid food May 1 and 2, were kept in isolation and no one bothered us, but most of us went through the mill with inoculation, vaccination and dysentery.

On May 26th I was put in the train for Mengede, walked to the mining village of Brambauer, given soup much better than previous, issued with trousers, cotton jacket, wooden shoes and foot rags and was down the pit by 10 that night. And what an experience. Being used to pits, this was no different, but the organization was far superior to any that I had known.

Away we went deep down into the bowels of the earth, about double the depth that I had been used to at home; then we were allotted out to German workmen, and for the whole of my working time in this pit, except for odd days when I deputized for absent German personnel, these two men were my companions, Gustave and Bruno, and they treated me like a son, never gave me anything, for they had nothing to give, but I worked with these two men all my months in these mines and we got on well together, and never was I bullied in any way. They guessed I knew mining, and I learned many things from these men, for it was entirely different mining, and I took a very keen interest in all that was undertaken.

"Gustave and Bruno I have never seen again or ever heard," Tom wrote later. "It has been one of my fancies to go back to Brambauer but it never materialized."

"We had a mutual respect, we and the German soldiers," said Tom as the interview neared its end. He still sat on the hard-backed chair where he had taken tea, and Mrs.

71

Easton lay on the sofa, deep into the evening paper. She had seen the paper boy coming and had hobbled to the front door to accept the paper from his hands. Now she read steadily, only occasionally glancing up through the curtains at the street outside.

"It was nothing like the civilian hysteria. There was a feeling of being set apart. When I was a prisoner, a German officer once came up to me and said, 'Fix that button.' I had a button undone. So I did it up. He was an officer and I was a private, and it didn't seem to matter that we were in different armies. We got along. We had to do the job, there wasn't much choice. I did get into a fight with one German artilleryman. Told me I was no soldier because I'd got myself taken prisoner. I told him he wasn't even in the war, being in the artillery. He wasn't on the line. Oh, we had some excitement then."

His eyes flashed. He grinned. "Sometimes we'd encourage scuffles between the Germans and the Russian prisoners. I only knew three expressions in Russian: No, Do you understand, and You're mad."

When the prisoners were released at the war's end, one of Tom's Russian friends gave him a treasured czarist shilling in return for all the food parcels he had shared with him. Even the Germans were envious of the way the British cared for their prisoners: private committees sent them special POW uniforms from England, along with tea and cocoa and a variety of tinned foods. One Sunday when the British prisoners were heating up their little coal stove and preparing a feast of meat and beans, a German inspecting officer came by.

"He nearly had a fit and swore. God damn, these lot are better off than us."

Tom's main interest at this time, however, was the quality of the German mines. He talked on for almost an hour about the advanced techniques, the pit baths (which were not to be built at the Northumberland collieries for decades), the special work clothes which the men removed after a shift and hoisted up on a pulley to be aired and dried, the token system that insured against a miner being left behind and also guaranteed that the first man down would be the first man up, the efficient construction of coal wagons, wheels flush to the sides, and so nicely balanced that a girl could tip them up to empty them. Electric lights were used long before they were in Britain, he noted, and the shoring system was safer too.

"The Germans used compressed air for everything. It was so much easier to work. We pit lads were experienced anyway, so we wouldn't have suffered in any kind of mine, but this was enlightening to us."

Mrs. Easton lifted her head. "He never had a chance to tell these things," she said. "Some of his ideas to modernize British mines."

Upon his return home, he told local mine officials about the German system, but nothing was done. Years later, he said, a Newcastle mine director went to Germany on an inspection trip and saw it was all true, what Tom had said, "and these things were finally done in the 1940s."

The diary: *On June 14th my toe was septic, mainly due to wearing wooden sabots, which took the skin off the top of the toes. So I was ordered to see the medical officer. I was ushered into the surgery and strapped upon a slab, and a nurse held my hands together. The doctor dabbed some cold solution on the toe, then took a scalpel and cut around one edge until he could get ahold of it, and he tore the whole lot off. I could have shouted to high heaven, but I contained myself. It was washed and dressed up, nurse released my hands and undid the straps and even shook my hand and said, Nice to see we still have some*

English men today. The doctor said, I know it is severe, but we find that the best cure. To cut it, you either go too deep or not deep enough, and when it is torn away it comes from a natural parting and you will not have any more trouble with it, and I did not.

August 9th I received my first letter from home, nearly four months after capture. At least they knew I was alive. . . . We had a British prisoner killed down the pit, his head crushed between two wagons, and we British prisoners that were available were present at the interment.

"Average death rates per year in mines over the period 1897–1911 were as follows: America, 3.31 per 1,000; Germany, 2.21; France, 1.52; Britain, 1.32."

***Mining: An International History,* John Temple**

On the last Sunday in October at church service the priest told us that the war was nearly at an end and the people of Germany had had enough, and that the Kaiser would be forced to abdicate in a matter of days. We went calmly on with all our work. Nov. 10th we were taken for a walk around the countryside by our commandant, visited eating houses and were treated very well. He also let it out that the war was to end tomorrow, Nov. 11th. The announcement brought joy to everyone, friend and foe alike. We were requested to carry on with our work until arrangements could be made for our release and care. We were told we could go if we liked. This we decided not to do. The Red Flag was hoisted on the mine shaft head. On Nov. 13th back-shift prisoners refused to go underground, and no force was used, and this terminated our term of prisoners of war. Nov. 17th a Farewell Night was indulged in by the Russians, Germans and ourselves, and on Nov. 18th we left in conveyances supplied by the mine owners and put on the train. . . .

In Rotterdam we were entirely kitted out in full army style with new uniforms, and we had many laughs at this: men of the Royal Naval

Division were counted as navy personnel and had to go to the navy department though they always wore soldier uniforms. They came back with a full naval rig, did not even know how to put them on, but we got them dressed up in comic opera style, and on 23 November we boarded the steamer *Willochra* and landed at Hull after a calm voyage.

Thousands of people greeted us as we arrived, and it was good to be back with wor ain folk. We were put on a train to Ripon and here again we had a grand reception, fully laid out meal for everyone, and nothing was spared. After a day or two, medicals and checking up, we were paid and granted two months' leave to our homes, and everything was done to see that we got there, and I quietly slipped back home to Bedlington Station and walked the rest of the way to my home in West Sleekburn. . . .

Eventually I was recalled to East Bolden, very few parades except to keep up a soldierly appearance. We were asked to fill in practice trenches at one of these camps, but we told the sergeant major that we had had plenty to do with trenches in the past years and it was not our intention to start to fill them in now, and we never did. Then we were pushed down to Ripon for the final hurdle, money in lieu of civilian clothes (£2 if you left your greatcoat) and finally put on Reserve Z and sent home for good.

The sum total of money paid by the Government to me for all these years of service, in the way of gratuities and paid leave after returning from Germany, which included my soldier's pay for the whole of my internment was £93–10–0.

My brother Joe, at the reception given by the Welcome Home Committee at the store hall, was presented with a solid gold inscribed watch for his honour in winning a military decoration in the field.

So now back to work for all of us. They took us all on at the colliery, but we had to accept what was available, and I was placed in the night shift, 4 to 11 P.M. When I had to present myself for interview before the colliery manager Mr. John Clough he casually said to me, Your father tells me you have just come from the German coal mines in Westphalia, how do you think they compare with the mining industry *in this country? Of course I studied it up a bit and asked him, Do you want a straight answer? Oh yes of course I do. Whereon I gave him this answer: You are 25 years behind the times.*

He nearly jumped over the desk at me. Nonsense, he said. I began then, for it mattered little to me whether he gave me a job or not, for I had not come back home to begin to beg for anything. I felt it and I knew it—I owed them nothing, nothing whatever.

I said, I have come from a group of pits which employs 1,200 at my pit alone, we have only one pony. You have 300 that I know of, employing about 500 men and boys all told. Never a hole is drilled by hand, but done pneumatically. Every person carries a completely safe electric lamp with rechargeable batteries at the lamp rooms. They operate pit head baths, both for male and female labor, a fully equipped operating theater is maintained at the surface, all personnel register themselves by the tally system—no shaft books go down the pit. Everything a miner required was available for him on the surface, temperance drinks, coffee, newspapers, clothing for underground use, soap, etc., few ropes were used for main haulage. They operated compressed air portable engines that could draw a set of 100 15-cwt wagons to the shafts. A safety device could arrest a cage in the shafts if the rope snapped (at that time totally unknown in England), all coal was ejected at the surface by compressed air power and done by women . . . . Motive power for winding was steam, but they operated huge condensers so that the water was used over and over again; no miner carried explosives, this was carried by one man who was the shot master, and I said if there is anything else you wish to know I can go on long enough. Where we do best them is quality; theirs is brown coal.

Needless to say, I was ushered out of the office to start work.

Temple: "Up to the mid-19th century Britain's position as the leading coal-producing country was unchallenged, but by the beginning of the 20th century Britain had been ousted from first place. 1912: America, 477 million tons;

Britain, 260 million; Germany, 172 million. Coal cutting machines were introduced only very slowly into British mines, whereas in American mines the opposite was the case. In 1913 only 8 percent of the total British output was mechanically cut, and this figure had only risen to 14 percent in 1921 and 31 percent in 1930. In America, 60 percent of the coal was mechanically cut in 1920 and the figure had risen to 78 percent in 1929. . . .

"In British mines almost all winding was done by steam engines; electrical winding before the 1920s was very exceptional. . . . As late as 1924 coal was electrically wound from only 182 British mine shafts. By 1912 more than half of British mines used no electricity to speak of."

"The mine in Blyth used to produce a million tons a year, but it's all gone now," Tom once told me. "It was beautiful coal, the vein was twelve feet thick. So black, and pure as pitch. I mourn it."

It was December when I saw Tom Easton again. A raw day, with lowering skies and a grim chill in the air. This time there was no rented car, and I made inquiries about local buses to Choppington, but the schedule was not encouraging, and since my train had been delayed an hour, I decided to take a cab. I knew that the Eastons would have been waiting and perhaps putting off their teatime for me, so it was with apologies that I greeted Tom at the kitchen door. He was undemonstrative, but I had a sharp sense of being more relaxed with him than before, partly because of the letters we had exchanged. On the back of his left hand he had written a telephone number—so he wouldn't have to look it up again when he got to the public booth where he made his calls. I handed over a tin of sweet biscuits and, muttering, "That's Mrs. Easton's department," he gave it to her in the living room. Later I noticed it, still in its cellophane, on the bedroom bureau.

The living room had been repapered. Oh yes, he had done it, with some help from his daughter: a professional job, too. In the tiny fireplace a coal fire glowed, and the room had the evocative coziness of some Beatrix Potter underground snuggery. While Tom hustled my overcoat into the bedroom, Mrs. Easton made conversation with a new easiness.

"The grandchildren call him Granda, you know," she said. "He takes them out riding, visiting relatives. Oh no, he doesn't have a car, never had a car. It's all the same. When you go, you canna take it with you."

As usual, Tom wanted to know about my schedule. I said I would see him the next morning and then again in the afternoon.

"What about lunchtime?"

Well, I wanted to go to the Morpeth library to do some research. Would pick up something there. See him later in the day.

He bristled. Just a little. "Spend the day here and not have lunch? I wouldn't hear of it. Couldn't allow it."

So that was settled, and now Tom, who had been restlessly prowling around his piano bench and his suitcase, beckoned me into the bedroom.

It couldn't have been more than nine-by-nine feet. There was barely a passageway between the bureaus, the large bed, tables and bookshelf, but everything appeared to be in its place. He ran a hand across the books: a set of Dickens, a Churchill or two, Lloyd George's memoirs,

The Compact Encyclopedia, the *New Illustrated Universal Reference Book,* war books, reference encyclopedias, gardening books, and *The World's Greatest Paintings.*

This last one he picked out and opened; the reproductions were excellent. "I saved for this," he said. "Surprising what a person can do if he doesn't throw away his money at the pub."

There was a bound volume of a veterans' magazine, "Twenty Years After": he and a friend taught themselves enough bookbinding to turn out a creditable job on it. He still pored over the old war maps and narratives, he added, and when he visited the battlefield he could speak with a certain authority.

"When I'm over there I stay with friends so I can come and go as I please. I get up around five in the morning, take an apple and an orange from the sideboard and walk about, I'm back by the time the others are finishing breakfast and just starting out. It's getting harder to go, now. I don't like to leave her, and she likes to bide at home. I do hope to get over in July of '76 for the sixtieth anniversary."

Once he heard a fellow veteran telling everyone where he had fought in the Somme action, even pacing off the line of his charge. "Why, the man was a mile away from where he said. I pulled out my maps and pointed to his unit there. 'Hoo did thoo know where I was?' he says. I knew, I knew."

Back in the parlor we settled into casual talk about the Easton family, the village, the past. Tom's grandfather died in his seventies, his father lived to be eighty-four, and Tom himself seemed barely affected by his years, so far as skin tone and energy and alertness. He did have all his teeth out some years ago "when they became carious, but I did it on weekends so I didn't lose a day of work."

He was never late to work, all his fifty-two years in the mines.

"We were born in a time when if you missed something, you missed it," he said. "Reliability counted for something. I did piecework in the pits from 1921 to 1961 and £12 a week was the most I ever made. (In 1952, his best year, his salary totaled £623.) That was as a top grade worker. It was lack of an education that held me down, you've got to have a second-class mining engineer certificate for the good jobs."

A charter member of the coal miners' consultation committee, he worked consistently toward nationalization of the mines, an issue so important to him that, when it was suggested to him that his aged father should dedicate the plaque celebrating the takeover, he didn't agree, for his father had done nothing for it. "You should have someone who worked at it," he said.

Before the owners installed baths at the pithead, washing was a major household operation. Outside every house in the row a huge washtub hung on the wall. ("You could be given directions by them," Mrs. Easton said. "You'd be told to look for the house with the green tub.") As a girl, she recalled, she used to earn pennies by scrubbing the backs of the menfolk in her family in Cambois, as they sat there in their shorts on a stool before the fire. (The stool more often than not would be a cockett, a low wooden table with two legs shorter than the others, used as an armrest when lying on one's side in the pit and working a foot-high seam; Tom brought out the cockett he had taken home from the West Sleekburn colliery when it closed in 1962.)

"Coal dust isn't so terrible as people think," Tom said. "Some of the lads didn't wash their backs, they thought it weakened the spine. Had a black area always in the middle of their backs."

Glimpses of a pit village: *Each house had a huge rain barrel, the softer water being used for personal washing and the clothes. (The only other source was the standpipe down the street.) Washing was a daily chore, when three or four men and boys had to be bathed in zinc bath tins set on the floor in front of the kitchen fire. Stockings and dirty vests were washed and dried ready for the next shift at the pit. Wet boots were cleaned by the womenfolk. There was little rest in these homes.*

Most families kept their own hens across the garden. Ducks were kept, also whippet dogs who took care of the rabbits in the countryside; this also added to the larder. Most women knitted all the pit stockings of heavy blue yarn, and all bread was baked at home, eight to sixteen loaves at a time. Herring were bought by the score and put down in salt or gutted and put on a long rod to dry in the sun. Mackerel were put down in tubs to pickle. In season we were up at dawn to collect mushrooms from the pasture land about us. These were made into sauce, or pickled. Boys attended to the blackberries in their season, and these were made into jams and jellies. Every person was industrious, young and old, male and female. Girls did all kinds of embroidery and needlework, and in the village there were dressmakers, perhaps a maid or a widow. Then there were the quilt makers, some of whom ran quilting clubs where quilts were made to order for neighbors who paid a certain sum each week. Men set up in the wash house as barbers, and we all went there for haircuts and many men for shaves. 2d for a boy's hair cut. One enterprising miner used to do fish and chips some nights, and he got our few coppers in the evenings.

One thing about having a pig was the smell, for no drainage was possible, but a cesspool was dug outside the sty and bricked up and a wooden cover put over it. We used to drain it with a pail and pour it down the drain. One thing about these drains, it was found that they led into pipes that went across the field two feet under the surface and ended there, had no outlet but just saturated the earth around, and no wonder we had a smallpox epidemic in 1906. The board went up outside the house as a warning and no one went near except the doctor; groceries were deposited on the step outside. There was one man with a horse-drawn ambulance who took all these patients to the hospital down by the river, and according to stories his only protection was ample supplies of whisky, and he was Alf Baldrey from the Millbank farm at Bedlington.

The co-op store played a big part in those days; everything was brought to the door, the butcher, baker, greengrocer, shoe repair van, and they were many times in the dark streets till 10:30 P.M. on Friday nights so that they got the money when it was available. Visits were made to the store during the week for smaller commodities, and credit could be given, for pay day came only once in two weeks, and the Saturday when there was no pay was called Baff Saturday.

Miners had to pay for all the powder they used. They made this into cartridges with newspapers. Deputies carried the detonators for these explosives, and they had a locked drawer fitted in their houses for the detonators.

The roads were made up nearly every winter by ash from the pit boilers which in summer was all right, but in winter it was ploughed up by heavy horse vehicles and the wheel tracks filled with water and the mess was dreadful. Lighting was there but in such small power in those days that they were only guide lights. We all made a brick track over to the wash house which kept things a little cleaner. We lived in a constant burning pit heap between the rows, always permeated with sulphurous smells depending on the wind.

The pig killings: *Times were hard in the pit villages at the beginning of the century, and families were often large, for a miner with four or five boys was always acceptable to the coal companies. Every colliery house in my village could boast a pig cree, the place where a pig was reared, brick-built, with an outrake where they were fed and cleaned.*

We schoolboys were always in touch with the pig killer, usually a miner, and each week in the frosty mornings we knew whose pig was going to be killed, which was usually before school time, and we would have our breakfast and go off with old Ralphie to the house who were having a pig killed. The pig always seemed to scent something, for when he went into the cree it usually squealed. They got the noose over the nose and led it out to the row, and then the killer got the big hammer and struck between the eyes and the pig went down stunned, and the knife was plunged into the jugular vein.

The women had their dishes ready and as the blood streamed in a helper kept it on the stir to prevent coagulation. Finally all the blood was drained and he was raised up onto the pig stool and boiling water poured over him. The hair was all scraped off, and next the stridlers blocked the pig on stretchers, head downwards, and again the sharp knives came out and cut the pig down the center to the forelegs, and all the organs were taken out into big wash tins and cleaned. Another stretcher was put in to keep the carcass open and it was left to hang there all day to dry out.

For all this we were awarded the bladder which lasted us two or three days as a football. We always had a broken clay pipe shank in our pockets to blow these up.

Those who had sent their offal to feed the pig were always sent some puddings and some ribs perhaps. Potted meats were also made up from parts of the pig, and these were also distributed. The hams were hung from hooks in the pantry ceiling and the sides rolled into bacon. Another piglet was got into the cree and the process went on. It was nothing for a pig to be 280 pounds in weight. This all finally ended with the passing of a slaughtering act, requiring a qualified butcher and licensed premises.

Old Alex Mole came down the pit one morning and found he could not pee, and had to return to the surface. He never came back, and I was asked to take over his work in 1921, and it was on a piecework basis, so wages went up a little.

To myself I had always promised to give my parents five years of work before thinking about setting out for myself. Of course I was developing girl friends, some from the war days who never had failed to write me, they were nice, but they were all engaged to this one or the other, so they went their ways.

After a few years a girl came to my home to see my sisters, and a feeling for her came to me and her for me, I believe, so this was developed, and she became my girl, and I never had any other.

My sisters both got married, Joe also courted a Cambois girl, and got married in 1920, and after a time transferred to work at Cambois pit. Finally I decided to ask Edith Lilian Patrick to marry me and was accepted, and we got a house at East Sleekburn before we married, and set this up to our satisfaction.

I got married at Cambois Parish church on June 21, 1924, by the Reverend R. Good, and after the reception etc. we went by train to Hawick, and we arrived there at 7 P.M. and stayed with Mrs. Stenhouse and had a very pleasant week, and I paid £2 for the whole week for us both, and we went straight into our own home and so on to the end of the year, when I recorded losing eleven days from sickness and five days for pleasure. . . .

Later Tom wrote me that: "Weddings went on all day, drinking and feasting, and all who were invited provided a present to the young couple which set them on their way to providing a home. Mats were made, and quilts, and all types of things were presented, pots, pans, kettles, teapots. This is how the colliery village helped in their community way. Halfpennies and pennies were collected weeks before by the bride's parents and the boys would all make a point of being just outside the church gates when these coppers were thrown out of the wedding carriage, and many times during the day we would assemble again and sing, 'Hey canny man, throw a hapenny out,' and they used to throw them out to watch the fun. Sometimes they heated them in a frying pan so that they were too hot for us to pick up, but we got our foot on them till they cooled."

My younger sister Ethel got married to Billy Gleghorn on the 1st of October, 1924, and they went to live at Bedlington in an upstairs flat, till she was taken to Princess Mary's Maternity Home in Newcastle on Feb. 27, 1925, and she went through an operation on the 28th, and on the 11th of March my mother and father were called away to Newcastle, and she died on the 12th of March. (Age: 19.) This was a very great shock to us all, and Edith had to go home and go to bed, for she was pregnant at that time.

Ethel was buried in Cambois churchyard on Sunday, May 15, 1925. The church was full, for everyone liked her. It was very sad for the husband and also for us. At that time a house had been bought for them at Stakeford so that Billy could be near his work as news agent at Stakeford, but no work was done in it. On the 20th of March Billy offered the tenancy of this house to me, and we straightway decided to take it as it was in grand condition, four-roomed house with scullery and big yard, also it had a bath fitted in. This became my home for the next ten years, had a good garden at the back.

On Sept. 29, 1925 my first baby was born, and I called her Ethel May Chisholm after my sister. . . .

And on to 1926, crisis year for the mining industry, for on May 3 we were out on strike on a question of hours and pay, and the slogan was, "Not a penny off the pay, not a minute on the day," and we went right through the summer, sometimes working very hard wresting coal from old pit heaps and sidings to keep the fires burning.

It was a glorious summer, and we were out as much as we could, even at six in the morning, away to some pit heap to get bags of coal, then wheel them home on a bike. We received strike pay of a few shillings a week and money from the National Assistance Board which was repayable, and this state of things went on till Nov. 29 when we again commenced work, but there were pennies off the pay and very, very many minutes on the day. But we demonstrated what we could do, and I believe it brought many changes from that time. A.J. Cook, the miners' dynamic Secretary at that time, came to East Sleekburn to talk to the miners on Sunday, July 6, and I doubt if that village has ever had a crowd like it before or since.

It was a sore drain on many families and us newly married people piled up debts for rent and were saddled with repayment scales. In my own case all these things were gradually paid back, which meant it was a great setback to married life for many years: make do with what you have, had to be our motto. Strike pay had run about 3 and 6 when you got it, and for December my total earnings were £10–15–0, and for the whole year my total earnings were £73–2–9. We redeemed all our debts by 1929.

"The movement which resulted in the General Strike of 1926 had been maturing for some time. Labor was irritated by the prospect of five years of Conservative rule, won by what seemed a dirty trick.... The housing shortage was still severe, the unemployment figures were high, and so was the cost of living. Then in July 1925 the Government subsidy to the coal industry came to an end. The mine-owners, in view of the continued low price of coal, gave notice that they intended to reduce wages, abolish the minimum-wage principle and enforce longer hours.

"The Miners' Union and the TUC took this as a challenge to declare the class war that they had now heard so much loose talk about, chiefly from Conservative papers. They threatened a coal and railway strike if the mine-owners carried out their intentions. The Government thereupon appointed a commission under Sir Herbert Samuel to investigate industrial conditions and meanwhile continued the subsidy. The Samuel Commission condemned subsidies, recommended that hours should be left as they were but that wages should be reduced, and proposed the collective selling of output and the closing of pits which did not pay their way. The mine-owners were constrained to accept this report. The miners rejected it with the slogan, 'Not a minute on the day, not a penny off the pay,' and were supported by a great number of other unions. The general feeling among working men was that Labour ought to show its gigantic combined power for once: not to punish or destroy but just as a warning that there were certain things that it would not tolerate. . . .

"On April 26th the miners ceased work. . . . The TUC then announced a general strike for May 3rd, to include all workers except those engaged in public health services. The day was awaited like a prophesied End of the World.

"It came. In London extraordinary things happened. All union labour went on strike. The Stock Exchange was feverish. Hyde Park was closed to the public and used as a milk depot. Troops were stationed in Whitehall and employed in convoying food. Public transport ceased completely—trains, omnibuses, trams, even taxis. But non-union business carried on, and thousands of office workers who could not cycle or get a lift in the crammed private cars walked 15 and 20 miles a day to and from suburbs. Many firms engaged rooms for their staffs in neighbouring hotels. The power plants were taken over by the Government, but illuminated signs were prohibited in order to conserve electric supplies. Fog added to the confusion. Soon amateur train, tram and bus drivers inaugurated a skeleton service. The material damage was considerable: it was not only that the strikers broke the windows of the scab vehicles but that the amateur drivers mishandled the engines from ignorance. . . .

"The Government was dealing successfully enough with the disorganization caused by the strike, the Labour leaders were wavering, the Samuel proposals seemed promising; the TUC therefore called off the strike on May 13th. Nevertheless the dockers, printers and transport workers remained out, in disgust, for five more days, and the miners for another six months. . . .

"The miners came off worst. That summer many of them were reduced to a diet of home-grown lettuce and stolen mutton from the hills. The coming of winter gradually forced them back to work; groups of them sued separately for peace with the mine-owners. Numerous poorer pits closed down for good, and unemployment among miners was so widespread that during the next few years the population of South Wales alone decreased by 250,000."

The Long Week-End, **Robert Graves and Alan Hodge**

1931: *I began to take an interest in the British Legion and was on the Committee, so this took me out one night in the fortnight. On Good Friday another baby girl was born and we called her Edith Lilian, baptized by the Rev. Good, vicar of Cambois, and she was a nice baby, but on May 4th, 1932, she died in Fleming Hospital at Newcastle after one day's illness, interred at Cambois churchyard alongside the graves of my brother Robert and sister Ethel. (Robert had "pined away and just died of a broken heart, I think" while his brothers were at the Front, 1917.) Again on Thursday Jan. 26th, 1933, our third*

*baby was born, we called her Isobelle. Ethel our first girl was now
attending Stakeford Primary School and doing all right. On April 24,
1934, our first baby boy was born, weighing 8 pounds and everything
was quite all right. . . .*

*My work with the Legion was increasing, also musical work. I
played with my Uncle Rob and his sons, and we had a group going
at West Sleekburn with the new undermanager, and we had practice
regularly, and I did all the gardens and work for Miss A.M. Coxon,
along at Bomarsund, so every minute of my day was taken up.*

*Nov. 4th Uncle White Patterson of Netherton was buried, this was
my mother's younger sister's husband. Mother and Barb attended, and
another well-known man in our village, Mr. James Beal, winding
engineman (and a very good one too) died in the bus, and I went to
the funeral on the 14th. (Margin Note: Joe Auld killed in the pit Nov.
14th.) And on the 16th Nov. our uncle William Smith died at
Bomarsund, my father's sister's husband. On the 20th I also attended
his funeral in Cambois, and to finish this chronicle of passings our
village schoolmaster, Mr. Joe Lenthard died while lacing up his shoes
on Christmas morning. He served with the Tyneside Scottish during
the war and I was also present at his interment.*

From a letter: "In the mining village when a death occurred, neighbour helped neighbour. Two men were
called to the home of the deceased and asked to be the
Bidders: their work on the day before the funeral was to
call at every house in the village and to say, You are
bidden to the funeral of our (brother or sister). Lift at 2:30
P.M., bury at 3 P.M. Six men were chosen as Underbearers.

"The following day the Bidders arrived first, then the
Underbearers. The priest or minister arrived. Then two
chairs were brought out into the street facing inwards.
The coffin was brought out, placed upon the chairs, pray-

ers were said, a hymn sung, the coffin put in the horse-drawn hearse, horse supplied by the coal owners, and all wended their way to the village churchyard. (Margin Note: The Underbearers were always offered a glass of whisky before going on their job, the only payment they had. This was always brought by the neighbour who was the helper for the day.)

"Before the mourners left the graveside, the undertaker would announce that all were invited back to the house for tea which had been prepared by the neighbours while everyone was at the churchyard.

"As old residents of the village pass away I attend if I can and record them as they go, but of course the old ritual has gone, with cremation etc. But a church service is usually held, even now, where we can attend, then it is left to the relatives to go to the committal. In the old days I have sung at hundreds of funerals; we were released from school to do so if we were in the church choir."

In 1936 the diary records that the Stakeford branch of the British Legion acquired a wooden building, formerly a double primary classroom, for £10 to use as a committee room. Tom helped dismantle it and bring it to a new site, and when it was rebuilt he put stencils around the walls above the dado rail. With a corrugated zinc roof, electric lights and a toilet added, the building was ready for a long service as Legion headquarters and a pivotal place in the lives of the village war veterans. Dances were held to help pay for the building.

We also trained a team of school children to do a Grand March at the beginning of the evening, and their parents had them all dressed alike, the boys with dark short trousers and white shirts.

In 1936 I did a lot of violin work one way and another for chapels, school dances and orchestral combinations. Also I did a great deal of work for Miss Coxon, both gardening, structural work and collecting rents at East Sleekburn, for down there, in conjunction with a jobbing bricklayer, we made waterclosets for the tenants. Total earning £152–18–3, sickness Nil, and so into 1937. (Margin Note: *Daughter Jane born Jan. 11, 1936.*)

Tom said his father taught him the violin. "We're a musical family," he added, rummaging around for a picture that eventually he produced, showing three generations of Easton musicians lined up in front of someone's house.

"I played with the Ashington bands and I used to be librarian for the village orchestra. Also a little group, the Fantasians. Did a lot of music for plays and operas, all through the second war."

The violin itself lay atop the piano. It was his father's, made by a ship's carpenter from Whitley Bay, he said, a beautiful job, with an inlaid throat. Conjuring up a jeweler's loup left behind by his son, Tom screwed it into his eye to study the maker's sticker inside but couldn't read it. "That must have been some ship's carpenter," he muttered. "I used to have a cello too, but she burned it." (A sly glance at his wife, who snorted.)

"What music? All kinds, I like all kinds, the serious stuff too. But not these off-chords, you know, a fifth and a seventh—it nearly makes you shiver to hear it." He chuckled. His Uncle Rob, "one of the biggest rascals that ever walked on two legs," used to string up his viola to the wrong notes (à la Paganini) so he could play apparently difficult passages with ease.

91

1938–1939: *July 30th was a Red Letter Day for miners for that was our first holidays with pay. The British Legion organized a trip to Glasgow. This was the forerunner of all the elaborate holiday arrangements that we know of today. We had the statutory holidays always, but this gave us Bank Holiday Monday plus two days, Saturday previous and the Tuesday for which we were paid, so actually it was a Red Letter Day for the mining fraternity. . . .*

Having been instrumental in getting my wife's father Jacob Patrick away on convalescence, we were astounded to learn on Oct. 30 that he had died at the home. So for the next three days I was excused my work and as the mother desired the body be brought home the duty fell to me to get all the necessary arrangements carried out. For a week or two I was a lot at Cambois to help my wife's mother get back to normal. . . .

The miners' picnic (1939) was at Morpeth on July 15th, and my daughter Ethel and myself went on our bikes. Aug. 2 marked a Red Letter Day for the Bedlington Coal Coy., with 100 years of mining, and they had built and opened 12 homes for retired miners at Bedlington. We all had a day's holiday with pay and a real sports day was arranged, with inter-pit competition.

Another remarkable change was, we enjoyed our first organized week's holiday. I worked my Saturday morning and also the afternoon shift, and I got the bus to London at 7:10 P.M., arrived at Victoria station at 8:15 A.M. and was met by Tom Dowsey's youngest daughter, who whisked me away to Thornton Heath for a quick breakfast. And what a reception I had from them all, for they had not seen me since their days in the colliery village of Craghead in County Durham, when I used to cycle across to their home and stay the weekend before their mother died. Then Tom Dowsey packed up and moved south to near Maidenhead, where he was in gentleman service, and met and married his second wife, and now they had set up a fish and chip business in Thornton Heath.

Tom had cycles ready, so we set off to Kew and arrived at his brother's house where we had tea, then we left and cycled all the evening, around to Maidenhead, and Tom collected a puncture, which we had to stop and repair, making us rather late. He had booked bed and food for us at a friend's who was a widow at Crookham, and we had to finish the ride in the dark. We finally landed in at 11 P.M., and the lady had gone to bed, but Tom got her up and she soon prepared us a lovely meal of ham etc., and how we did set about it, for we were both very hungry, and it was not long before we rolled in. This was my first sleep since 2 A.M. on Saturday. Our old Battalion motto was "Harder Than Hammers," and we must have been.

We made our way to Windsor, where we had a look in the castle grounds, and off to Hampton Court and after a look around there, set off via Runnymede to Kingston and thence back to Thornton Heath at 10 P.M. where we had to nearly fall off our bikes. I was not long in being off to bed.

Tom had business to attend to the next day, and Mrs. Dowsey put up sandwiches for me, and I set off cycling to Epsom and Guildford and back, a bit stiff but in good trim.

"Once I was on a bike trip in 1939," Tom recalled, "and I met a tramp by the side of the road. I'd been given lots of sandwiches by my hostess, a liberal woman, so I said, Sit down and we'll have a good feed. I asked him why he was a tramp, and he said he'd been injured and couldn't get steady work, so he went about from one workhouse to another working as he could."

The following day I made my way by train to London, to where my wife's sister Isabelle and her husband lived. We had a meal and talked late into the evening, and I stayed the night there. Returned to Thornton Heath, and the following day saw me on the road again with the bike. Cycled all day and had a good meal, after which I offered to take both my host's daughters to the pictures at Granada. The following day was out shopping to get a few presents, packed my bag and left my friends at 6 P.M., traveled all night, arrived at Stakeford at 7 A.M. and rested for that day, was back to work on Aug. 14 at 2 A.M. Holiday pay paid £2-15-0.

By August 25 there was a great fear of war and feverish prepara-
tions were being made, on Wednesday practised with the Fantasians,
and we provided the music for the flower show held in the recreation
grounds at Bedlington Station until 6 P.M. Then on Sept. 3rd a state
of war declared between ourselves and Germany from 11 A.M., and
so the clouds of war began to gather again in our country.

Then the miners began to lose days off work for various reasons, loss
of contracts, shipping movements and general concentration on provid-
ing the fighting forces for the country, and on October 14 there came
another severe blow to our sea power, for the Ark Royal was sunk at
Scapa Flow.

During the slack days I made enough whist tables to carry on whist
drives in the Legion Hut to raise revenues. . . . Mrs. White was killed
on the Stakeford Road by being knocked down, which has been put
down to the complete blackout and people walking on the road and not
the footpath, for motorists' lights had to be screened.

Seeing the pits were not doing too well, when I was over at Ashing-
ton one day towards the end of 1939, I popped into a recruiting office
and offered to join the army, with a view to asking for the Pioneer
Corps, where I felt I could do a good job, quickly rise in rank, being
well conversant with army procedure.

All went well until they came to my occupation. Then the papers
were scrapped, for at that time there was no recruitment of miners other
than reservists, so I came home and said nothing more about it. And
on to the end of 1939, the year the lights went out again, and it was
many a year before they were relighted.

One afternoon after a long conversation about Tom's
family I tried to switch abruptly back to the morning of
July first. He still hadn't told me what was going through
his mind during that nightmare march across No Man's
Land, and I thought that if I kept coming back to it I might
surprise a sudden remembering of how it was.

I got another kind of surprise. For the first time since I had met him he bristled and growled. "What, that?" he snapped. "Well, ask me quickly." Turning away truculently, he muttered, "Write me your questions after. I'm tired of talking about the war."

1940–1941: *On May 22nd I was called to an interview with Mr. George Atchison, colliery undermanager, who had been given the command of the local defence volunteers, and I was immediately accepted as a leader and the following day was present at Bedlington Police HQ with Herbert Laws, and we collected denims, rifles for the force and brought them to West Sleekburn. HQ was set up in the first aid room and the lamp room, and on the 24th guards were mounted against parachute troops. I did my first spell of duty from 8 to 10 P.M. in charge of the guard.*

On the 25th we went to Bedlington with the defence force and paraded, and I found that my brother Joe was also there as a leader from Cambois, so we were together again, in uniform, working in the same line, signals.

Friday 14th of June, 1940, a sad day. Paris fell to the Germans without a fight, and the Germans occupied that city. July 6th the Pit was laid idle through air raid warnings being sounded, but I was called to work at 1 P.M. for essential duties. This brought other agreements into force with the colliery owners, and we never laid the pit idle any more because of air raid warnings. Sometimes work ceased for awhile, and in later days we never stopped at all, we carried on as if they were not there. . . .

David Phillips, another of our surface workers, had to report (to the army) on the 12th of September, so we were very short-handed, and we worked three double shifts a week, 2 A.M. to 5:30 P.M., and this went on for weeks on end. It nearly always fell to my lot to also do this on Saturday, on-shift coal drawing and after that, attention to shaftwork and repairs, a very heavy task with all the other commit-

ments that we had in the defence field, but we carried on.

We were put through exams for the purpose of testing skill and knowledge of army signals, and I was unanimously passed as OK. I was offered the post of Signals Officer to the 14th Battn. Home Guard, with the rank of lieutenant, and I accepted, so from then my role changed. I was no longer to be with the West Sleekburn Company. Guard duty ceased for me, but was with the Battalion HQ staff.

In the early part of 1941 I was doing three or four nights upon Home Guard training, having a signal section at every company plus Battalion HQ which was first centred on a shop at Glebe Row, Bedlington. Then we moved to the disused public house at the other side of the road, the Turks Head. Companies were located at all the villages, and most had a few men training in signals, and it was the coordination of these groups that occupied my mind. At first I traveled all these places in turn on a push-bike in all weather, and it was a tough job. . . .

A man called Harris was killed by a mine at Cambois, and a soldier the same day, mines coming adrift and washing onto the beach.

Tom never got a medal, his wife remarked; never was made even corporal during the first war, though his responsibility was known and relied upon time and again.

"Well, they made me a lieutenant in the Home Guard," he retorted.

"And so they should."

"I was in charge of eight signal companies," he told me. "I cycled around to all eight on schedule on my push-bike, though it meant that the following day I'd work only one shift, from 9 A.M. to 5:30 P.M. I often worked a double day, and Saturdays I worked 4 A.M. to 4 P.M. Sundays I would be off, but I'd spend all day at the firing range, then up at 2:30 A.M. Monday. You add it all up, the fifteen hours three days a week, the twelve on Saturday, the normal shift on two days and it comes to seventy-four hours a week. I never saw my family from one week to another."

"And it was heavy manual work, mind," added Mrs. Easton.

Tom's arms bulged massively under his cardigan. In his prime he stood 5 feet 6 1/2 inches and weighed close to two hundred pounds. Hands: square with somewhat short but articulate fingers. On the left wrist was a scar made by a chisel which he drove to within a millimeter of the artery. (That time, holding the wrist pressure point, he managed to get from the work shed to the house, slip on a jacket and walk up the street to the doctor's without his wife knowing anything was wrong. He was pleased that the accident didn't cost him a day of work.)

1941–1942: *Feb. 16th had a seven-hour air raid warning. That week it hardly ceased snowing, the worst I had ever known. I had to work double shift as those who had to travel did not turn up for a week. On the 19th my father was not too well and could not go to work, the first time this had happened since the days of his accident.*

In 1908 Tom's father was crushed by a loaded tub being drawn by a runaway pony in the mine. He suffered severe abdominal and spinal injuries but recovered. For ten days Tom and the other children were farmed out to uncles and aunts, and a collection was taken in the village to enable two uncles to stay off work and sit up nights with the victim.

20th: *never ceased snowing; no newspaper, telephone lines were down all over the country, still we carried on with the Home Guard from 8 to 10 P.M. On the Friday we called for our pay but no pay was available, just subs for those who could not manage without their pay over the weekend. The Pit was idle on the Monday and we were*

*paid on the Tuesday. During all this time we kept the work of the
British Legion going. . . . The electric current failed, and we had great
difficulty getting men out of the pits. 1941 was a very heavy year at
work for we worked with one man short right up to Sept. 1st. There
was an RAF plane down in the Long Riggs, dismantled and taken
away by the RAF. About this time we got delivery of wireless sets for
the Home Guard, another innovation that required special training.*

*That year we commenced conveyor working at the pit, and this began
the increases in production; soon output began to creep up and up, and
little knowing it at the time, a revolution in mine working was taking
place, not only at our pit. . . .*

*Feb. 21, 1942, I represented the British Legion branch at the
North Eastern Area Conference in Newcastle; on the Sunday was at
Dr. Waterhouse's residence in Bedlington for practise to provide the
music for a play put on by the local dramatic society. Feb. 28th was
my father's last day at work, at the age of 72, completing over 61 years
of service to the Bedlington Coal Company. He was given a small
pension, coal as he wanted it, and allowed to remain in the coal
company house for his life time.*

When Tom himself retired after his fifty-two years, the
mines had long since been nationalized. He was a charter
member of the consultation committee, the miners' union
contact with the government, and for years this group had
pooled its small fees to provide parties and commemora-
tive plaques for retiring workers.

"I didn't get a party," he said. "I wouldn't have the local
pit official do me the honors, I thought it should have
been someone on the National Board. So it just never
happened. I got the £200 retirement award, but I never
did get the cardboard."

The same quietly stubborn self-assertion could be seen,

incidentally, in the way Tom gave up smoking. It happened in 1931.

"I smoked a little, you know. Smoked a clay pipe. It wasn't allowed in the pits, but many did it on the sly. One day I had a confrontation with a guy, he'd just given me a scare and I told him to look sharp or he'd kill someone through his careless ways and it would probably be me he kills. So the guy came back at me. Threatened to report me for smoking."

The reminiscent smile faded. "I said, 'You'll never have another opportunity.'" The voice: cold, level, deliberate. "I stopped right there and then. Never smoked again to this day. It's easy when you have a reason."

I thought about that remark later. It was a telling indication of something hard in his personality, not exactly vindictive, but unrelenting: he could have been a fanatic, perhaps, with a different background. This bitter tenacity, I felt, was the underside of Tom's rocklike reliability.

5 March 1942, another Red Letter Day: *canteen facilities start at the Pit so that food could be had while at work, and it relieved the strain on the rations at home. On April 10th we got another piece of furniture, a Morrison Air Raid Shelter, and I erected it in the kitchen below the kitchen window, and it was used as a table when not doing duty as a shelter. . . . 18th of April saw another fatal accident at the colliery. Oswald Davis, a coal cutter, was crushed to death between the cutter and the roof, and again on May 17th a chargeman was killed. We were on parade at the Pit premises when news came of this accident: Reginald Young, he was one of my signalers, so I waited around until he was brought to the surface. . . .*

I have not mentioned that I worked 300 square yards of garden over on the river side; this I did whenever I had a spare moment and managed to always have it full to meet the household needs in flowers and vegetables. . . .

Rather reluctantly I have to record that our first officer commanding the Home Guard battalion, a grammar school master, was court-martialed for the misuse of army funds. He was cashiered and ordered to serve twelve months hard labor, but six months of the sentence was remitted by the King. The funds mainly went in providing drinks etc. wherever he traveled.

On a field training expedition during which Tom got to sleep in a bell tent again "along with Jack Oliver, who lost his leg with us on July 1, 1916," he decided to spend some free time visiting his wife's aunt in Shiremoor, close by the hotel which was to be his headquarters as umpire of some military exercises.

"Lieutenant H. Barnes and myself walked across to see her in the evening, and later there was an air raid warning, so we stayed beside her until it was over. We walked back after midnight, and we tried the hotel door but it was locked, so Harry and myself went further up the road, got into the grass hedge, made ourselves comfortable with our greatcoats, and we slept there till the early morning. At dawn we were down to the cookhouse of the Camerons and had the first tea that was made and a good breakfast also."

1943, the year of the motorcycle: *They took our iron palings away from our gardens for the war effort. . . . (Margin Note: was raised to the commissioned rank of captain.) Was again up to see the CO and he said, For the past two years you have cycled around on a* push-bike, around the whole of Bedlingtonshire, and you just cannot keep all this work up and do this, so I propose to indent for a motor car for you. Can you drive a car?

I said, I have never had a chance to try, Sir, and I would like to suggest something else. Well what's that? I have four 350-cc Matchless motorcycles under my charge which are very little used except on exercise and they are brand new. I would prefer to take one of these. I can house a motorcycle when I cannot house a car.

Right, he said, you take your choice, for you cannot be allowed to work yourself to death the way you have been doing. . . . On the 3rd of June my younger brother Edwin and I went up to the Turks Head and selected the motorcycle that I wanted, and I got on the pillion and off we went. At East Sleekburn I said, Stop here, and when he stopped I said, Tell me how to do, and he went on the pillion and I rode the motorcycle home. He came one other time with me, and from there I rode on my own, never any more tuition did I have, and that was my constant companion until the Home Guard stood down. The whole aspect of my work changed, companies were contacted in no time, I could move men from one place to another to take up duty, and so the push-bike got the go-bye. Later I got despatch rider's clothes, crash helmet, gloves and wellington boots. . . .

On June 5th Mam was up to Thropton to satisfy herself where Ethel was working (in domestic service), and on the 13th she was home here to tea with a friend and stayed overnight; she decided to join the Women's Land Army. . . . I went with her to Newcastle, for she had to report to the Whalton hostel.

In November we took over the vicarage at St. John's Bedlington Station and used this as a battalion school at weekends. Gave a lecture there on communications. 2nd December, Ethel was down again home for a few rest days, liked her job with the W.L.A. . . . Continued on Exercise Tweed until the 30th; on the Monday had to report on the exercise, and in that week did three nights for the Home Guard, one for the band, and after work on the Saturday went home and had a rest.

1944, the accident: *Feb. 28, 1944, had to report for Company C conference at the Battalion School, but I never got there. It was a black frost, and as I approached the bottom of Bomarsund colliery houses a big dog ran slap into my front wheel and turned the handlebars, and I was pitched over the side into the road, the bike on top of my leg.*

I lay a minute or so, then not being able to feel any great injury I managed to struggle from under the bike. People had heard the clatter so they came out. One happened to be Joe Clark, a cornet player who used to come to the band, so I asked if he would push my bike into the backyard and let it stay there until called for. He insisted on seeing me to Doctor Brown, surgery, for he would still be busy, so I walked there and saw my old friend Dr. H.S. Brown, and he said, Now Tom what is the matter? Whereon I told him and said, The only thing that I can feel is perhaps a broken rib, as I had a little difficulty with deep inhalation.

He said, We'll see. So clasping me around the chest he began to squeeze. Does that not hurt you? he said. I said, No. Right, he said, go home, you have no broken ribs.

So I walked down home, was much bruised and went to bed. Had to make arrangements to stay off work. Managed to get up the next morning and get down the stairs, but I was very sore and could not move around, so managed on the settee. Doctor called and examined me and said, You ought to be in bed. And to that I said, Well I am NOT GOING. Oh, said the Doc. That's Doctor's orders. But I replied, I don't care whose orders they are, I stay here, nobody is going to run up and down the stairs after me. I can creep to the toilet and I am taking no harm where I am, so that was that.

Got my situation reported to my O.C. and he visited me on March 1st, saying, Knew something drastic had prevented you from turning up on parade, so I just had to rest. . . . My brother Edwin popped along and brought the bike home, no damage done, just bent footrest. Had a slow walk up to see my parents at the top of the avenue; as my brother Joe was here to see me, he gave me a helping hand. . . . On the 25th

*March I got signed off by the doctor and commenced my work on the
27th in the back shift, and from then on progressed back to normal.
My work being all day heavy muscular work and piece work, I could
not start to be a drag on my marrows, and this never did happen.*

Miners worked in pairs or sometimes foursomes, called
marrows, and a man might spend his entire working life
alongside the same marrow. Once Tom showed me a picture of Harvey Laws, his marrow for many years, long
since dead. Laws had a heart condition and moved very
slowly, stooped over because of his height. When Tom
was still quite young a foreman took him aside and
pointed out that Tom was beginning to walk that way
himself. It took no little effort to break the habit.

*May 18th Ascension Day, Bobby Bell was killed in the Pit, the
son of the village postman. We finished work at 9 A.M., no back shift
turned in. June 4th, Sunday, Sheila Brown of Amble, Ethel's friend,
died, only very young. Tuesday, June 6th, D Day. The attack on the
continent commences at dawn and was going quite well, and we gained
and established a foothold in Europe again. Ranked to be one of the
biggest military operations ever undertaken and a triumph in organization. Wed 7th, Ethel came and her mother was with her to Amble for
Sheila Brown's funeral. . . .*

Perhaps we talked too long that evening. At least I was
exhausted, and the edge of my hand was blue with
smeared ink. Without much ado I left, Tom accompany-
ing me again to the bus stop where I took the local to
Morpeth. Darkness had fallen, and the rain was so heavy
I could hardly tell where to get off. Having made no
reservations, I had to try three places before I found a
room, just off the triangular space that is the center of
town, with an ancient tower at its base, around which cars
had to maneuver single-file. The barman said Morpeth is

a handy stopping point for salesmen working the eastern parts of the county.

In the morning the rain still sluiced down relentlessly. The street outside was full of umbrellas and slickers, and passing cars had their windshield wipers on at high speed. The only other guest in the breakfast room was a shiny-haired young man who had set an electric heater before his feet. We talked across the room while we waited for our bacon and eggs.

He told me of his cousins in Canada and of his job with Shell Oil in Scotland, and naturally the conversation got around to accents. The Geordie accent was the toughest of all, he said.

"You know how the Geordies got their name?" he asked.

I had no idea, unless it came from a movie I saw years ago about a Scottish hammer-thrower.

"It was in the early days of the mines. They're all pit lads, the Geordies. There were two safety lamps, came out about the same time. The Davy lamp and another one invented by George Stephenson, the railroad man. Well, Stephenson came from the north country, so the northern lads wouldn't go down the pit wherever they were working, Wales, anywhere, unless they had Geordie Stephenson's lamp. He was one of their own, see. So people took to calling the lads Geordies too."

1944, the war winds down: *Sunday, Sept. 24th, Wm. C. Osborne died. He lost a leg with us in the Tyneside Scottish on July 1st, 1916, and he worked in our powder magazine at the Pit. He kept up his association with the 4th Bn. Tyneside Scottish by attending all the dinners, also he had always been a member of the British Legion. So on the 27th we attended his funeral, representing both organiza-*

tions. On Oct. 3 I called upon the widow to see if there was anything that we could do for her.

From 24th Sept. as our bridgehead on the Continent was firmly established, we began to take in Company lines etc. from the instructions received. Stores were gradually brought back to Battalion HQ and checked.

My practise with the bands still carried on throughout the year each Wednesday night. Sunday we were out and took lines down from the bunker at Bedlington, and gradually parades became fewer and fewer. On Nov. 1 we got the order for the stand-down of the Home Guard, and on the 2nd I took my brother Edwin to Bedlington and he handed in all his despatch rider's clothing.

On the 6th of November I took the shelter out of the house, which had stood in good stead many a time for my wife and children. It gave a certain amount of comfort to them during raids for they knew it was calculated to withstand the masonry falling on them if the house was shattered, but we were never very near to that point. One German bomber was shot up and came down at the brickworks at Bedlington Station, and a land mine was dropped one night at Newbiggin. Two houses were shattered at Bedlington Station and Ravensworth Terrace, and a bomb dropped at Ballast Hill in Blyth, so the shelters were dismantled and stood outside to await collection.

Collected Ethel at 9 P.M. at Guide Post; she brought me a new hedge knife bought through a farmer for which I paid 10 and 6. Sunday 12th we took in more telephone cable and down home at 1 P.M. 14th, annual meeting of the British Legion and afterwards they presented me with the stove from the HQ, and I set it up in my workshop at the foot of the garden.

Sunday, 19th of November saw the last parade of the 14th Bn. Home Guard. . . . Ethel home for her week's holiday from the Women's Land Army. Young Jack Godsmark a few doors up the avenue was killed in the Pit at the bottom of the yard seam drift by runaway tubs. His parents were in a very grieved state, only just in his 20s and a noble lad. . . . 18th December I was up to Mother's and it was proposed that I take the family piano down to my home as I had four children and it would help any of them if they desired to take up learning. Had to await the consent of the others in the family.

Total wages 1944, £307–12–0. Received from the Home Guard loss of earning for accident £15–18–0, four weeks at £3–18–6 a week. . . .

1945: *April 15th my wife and I were at the Central Hall, Ashington, to hear Marie Wilson on the violin and other celebrities, and we walked home that night, too late for the last bus. April 28th was up at my sister Barbara's who was ill in bed and sat with her awhile and was back again on the Sunday to see her, still very poorly, but we talked and she said she felt better, but the next day they came and sought me, for my sister was dead. She was buried in Cambois churchyard; on the Sunday following we were at church with other members of the family, for this was generally the custom after a bereavement in pit villages (that is, for the family to attend church in a group). Doctor came at 1 P.M. and made a thorough examination of my wife, who was not too well over a period of many weeks. 7th, all armed resistance of the Germans ceased. May 8th VE Day and the Pits were idle for this momentous occasion when the whole country was relieved from the spectre of war in Europe, but there were other spheres to be cleared up. My wife went to Newcastle today to see the specialist and was admitted to the Royal Victoria Infirmary and underwent an operation on the 17th May and her condition was said to be comfortable.*

My wife was out of bed on May 30, perhaps a bit shaky but she kept out of bed. . . . During these months I was up to see my Mother as much as possible, for she got out very little now.

The Eastons' 1945 vacation: *My wife went to Rothbury and managed to get rooms booked for us on 25th July, and on the 28th we all got settled in. Wages that week were £6–5–0 plus £5–15–0*

*holiday and a shilling tax refund, and this is what we had to provide
a holiday for two adults and three children, but we managed and
enjoyed every minute. My wife's cousin Bess lived there, married to
a shepherd, so we tramped the Cheviot hills while Mam kept her cousin
company.*

*. . . 20th December, on this day was put on the Branch Committee
of the Trade Union at the Pit. Christmas day in this year was the
poorest we had ever had in six years of war. Friday 28th over to the
union hut and sorted out membership cards. Total wages £315–1–0
and not one day lost in sickness, entering 1946 and leaving behind
war connections etc., it proved that I was busier than ever and this year
was packed full of decisions one way and another.*

Remembering that first summer when Tom was out of
school, I asked him if he had ever thought what would
have happened to him had the colliery manager not spotted him. The notion seemed hard for him to grasp, but
finally he said he might have gone into clock making,
which had always been one of his boyhood interests.

"When I was a kid I fixed a clock in the house, got it
going all right, but I broke a tooth of a gear, and soon it
went wrong again. So a friend of my mother, who was a
clock maker, looked at it and he said, 'Whoever fixed this
did a good job on it, mind, but I got to say this, it was a
valiant effort for someone who knew nothing about the
subject.' "

Tom and his wife served as unofficial agents for their
son, collecting broken clocks and watches from neighbors
to be picked up by Bill on his way into Newcastle. When
I was at the house somebody dropped a clock in through
the mail slot. Tom inspected it. "Well," he muttered, "if
it didn't need fixin' before, it does now."

"My Life in the Mines," a letter from Tom: "The crackett we talked about was always set out by the mother, and all your gear put upon it ready for you to don in the morning. We were worked at various boy-jobs for 10 hours a day and all mealtimes deducted from that, the owners maintaining we were only working 8 1/2 hours a day. Now, we were only allowed to work 42 1/2 hours in a week, and the pit worked six days a week. So on one day during the week we were sent home at the dinner break and those remaining hours were worked on a Saturday.

"Off I went at 6:30 A.M., of course we were just little slaves, for I had to come back home at 8:30 to 9 for my breakfast, then at midday to 1 P.M. for dinner and finish at 4:30 P.M.

"You stayed at that work (mostly sorting coal or tipping—dumping—the tubs full of coal as they came up from the pit) until you got used to tubs and all the safety measures guarding against injury etc., and learned some pit sense.

"I worked on the surface till I was 15, and then I was agitating to get down the pit. You could go underground then if you were 13 years. Now, the underground boys only worked eight hours and had a little higher pay, so there was always this draw to get underground, but I stayed on the surface till I was coming up to 16 years. Having some education and very adaptable, I was put upon jobs which required this type of lad. Our wages were raised in accordance with our age, each year a slight advance, not much but it was there.

"1911, Coal Mines Regulation Acts, introduced into Parliament by a Labour member of the House, became law, and many great changes and improvements came as a result: eight-hour day (no meal time excluded) underground and eight hours twenty minutes surface. We came to weekly payments and worked only one shift each Saturday. Previously we worked two shifts every other Saturday, 3 to 10 A.M. and 8 A.M. to 3 P.M., so all football matches were held after 3 P.M. on the Saturdays in mining areas. (Sports—we never did much. Threw a ball around, a bit of football. I played for the church team awhile. There was no time for sports when we were lads. . . .) Underground, we drove pit ponies hauling coal to the pit shaft. They classed you as drivers. When youths got older they could put in for 'putting,' which meant they were cavilled (selected by lot) and took whatever seam and district in the mine that came out of the hat. They were paid at a piecework rate. This also applied to the 'hewers' fraternity, but you could not graduate to hewing until you were an adult and had passed through the various stages.

"Hewing was in the main piecework also, gauged by the thickness of seam in which they worked, the narrower the seam the higher the price per ton, and these people hewed a ton of coal for 10d a ton, sometimes from a vein only two feet thick.

"Hewers were hewers of coal and nothing else: the prima donnas of the job. Putters had to work when the hewers were at work, to get the coal away from them down the roadways thence to the shafts. Putters with their ponies had to work at times in 3 feet 6 inch high spaces, crouched over their work most of the time. Their tubs got off the rails very very easily, through earth movement and bad joints, so they had to be strong to put a 10-cwt tub back on the rails. They worked by themselves and their pony.

"We never worked three shifts coal producing like some other mines—only two. The third shift, 6 P.M. to

2 A.M., stonemen worked in the stone following the roadway in to keep pace with the coal working, blasting in tops to make headroom and taking out bottom stone for the same purpose. Of course, all this is now changed in mechanical mining.

"My father did not wish me to go putting, so I finally got to rope haulage. We used a lot of endless ropes for haulage over longer distances, and we older boys were suitable for this work, having to work on our own and use signaling equipment. I was at this stage in 1914, then just turned 18 years, and being used to signaling equipment brought me into that part of the army.

"When I got home from the war, a new generation had sprung up and they were jealous of their jobs, so the returning heroes had to take night shift for the time being at least. This meant going to work at 4 or 6 P.M., and that did not fit the bill for a young man of 22. I began to protest and finally was brought to day shift work as rolleywayman, where I had a whole district to maintain in haulage rails, which we called rolleyway, also in charge of the pony drivers etc. We learned the art of steel rope splicing, which had to be carried out with endless ropes, and after awhile a vacancy occurred for an onsetter, which meant you loaded all coal at the pit bottom into the cages for its journey to the surface, and here you worked in a group, which again incorporated signals.

"(When I was given the work there was a deputation to the management asking why I should get this job. I told them that I did not see any of them at a deputation in France when I was doing that job. They were flat.)

"Very heavy muscular work this, for it was all handwork and this incorporated bringing all materials down the shafts on an overtime basis: rail, pipes, girders, ponies, anything that could not be handled during coal-drawing hours. We did coal-drawing in eight-hour shifts and scarcely ever ceased: a cage a minute traveling up and down 120 fathoms.

"After 10 years I was brought to the surface to do the same work at surface level, and this I maintained until I retired in 1961. In the last four years of my work we were given mechanized means to do this work, so although 65, I could do just as well as anyone, so I did 40 years of piecework, paid by the effort involved. I attained the certificate of deputy overman.

"My father always maintained my work did not utilize the knowledge that I had, nor my intelligence, so to satisfy him I took mining lessons and attained my certificate to assure him I did possess these capabilities, but they did after all stand me in good stead when the Coal Board was instituted and I was put on the Consultative Committee. I was offered official jobs later but declined them."

"One summer in the fifties I went to Oxford," Tom said casually. "It was a summer school at Jesus College arranged through the National Coal Board. I studied industrial relations there, and this helped me later, I suppose, when I was chairman of the miners' lodge. I'll say one thing, I've seen better beds on the coal face than a poor lad's bed at Oxford."

The Labour Party also sent him to a summer school at Beatrice Webb House in Surrey one year.

Working on overtime: "Conveying any long material down the pit, such as pump pipes eighteen-feet long, involved standing in the shaft on top of the cage and pushing the pipes down through a trap door in the cage roof. When we got six or eight on we strapped them together, fastened this to the cage chains, and two men put their arms around them to steady them and rode with them to the bottom of the shaft. There we untied them and slid them out singly onto the flatsheets, but most of the time we clattered them all out together and away back to the surface for another load, while the men at the bottom lifted the ones we dropped and packed them on a tram. This type of work was carried out most nights after our ordinary coal-drawing work, and it gave us a little extra money."

Evening gloom had made us all dim figures to each other before Tom turned on the lights in the little living room. I suggested he might want to get ready for his evening meeting, but he insisted there was plenty of time. We talked of children.

"It was diligence and hard work," he said. "We brought them up with the [Episcopal] church; they weren't spanked. I never was much for makin' a lot of noise. One time I had a fight with my brother Edwin, ten years younger than me and livin' in the same street. Some letter that was for him was delivered at our house and opened by mistake. It was something personal, and we sent it on to them, and then Edwin and his wife made a fuss. They came to the house, and Edwin's wife refused to come inside but stood outside the door raising a fuss. I told him, 'There's never been so much noise in my house as this. Never. A simple word is enough.' "

As he said it, his face tightened slightly, not with anger but with a kind of sad resignation.

"Never has any of my children back-answered. It

wasn't done by any threat, just by the observance that someone is right and fair."

He said, "I never enter my children's homes to this day, unless invited."

A letter from William Easton, Tom's son: "During my childhood I did not see a lot of my father. He worked in the mines during the day and also worked in shifts, going out during the evening and working through to morning. When not in the mines he was on duty as a captain in the Home Guard. He rode a motorcycle around the area carrying despatches.

"He has always been a keen gardener and spent a lot of time in his garden. Growing things has always held a special interest for him, and even now he shows great fascination for new varieties of flowers and vegetables. This is one of the many things I have inherited from him, and he still spends all his free time in his garden. This I think is his greatest pleasure.

"As a family we spent a lot of time visiting other members of the family during the war days, and this was enjoyed by my three sisters and I. Dad was a great believer in family visiting and still is. We had a family holiday each year in the country, not far away from our home. We spent our time walking in the countryside and made a collection of wildflowers picked from the hedgerows.

"Dad was not a strict parent in the respect of telling you what to do and expecting you to do it his way. He would always give advice and guidance, but the decision would be left entirely up to yourself. He never said you should not do a certain thing but would encourage you to his way of thinking. He believes all things are perfectly all right in moderation, and although I am a pipe smoker and also take a drink, it does not alter any relationship between us. Advice was always given but not enforced.

"My occupation came to me during a period when he was doing work in other services, and in fact was seeking a watch to be presented to a nurse. He had a chat with the manager of a jeweler's about apprentices, and I was interviewed for the post and started work the following week. The family were all very happy about this and probably more especially Dad, as he has also a great interest in the mechanics of watchmaking and clock repairing. Which he really picked up himself over the years, and even now thinks nothing of repairing a clock. I shall forever be grateful for the door he opened for me in this field.

"During my two years of National Service I had time to read and understand what a source of knowledge this man had. He is a magnificent letter writer. As a family we attended church regularly, and we were brought together in my absence by tuning in to the radio on a Sunday evening for Songs of Praise. Our thoughts were always with each other at that time.

"He does not get agitated very often, but can do. If for instance one commences to do a job or chore of his own in his absence and does not complete it, he can get agitated on his return. For although he has spent a lot of time doing public work he has never once neglected a single chore or duty to his home or family. His planning is so intense, he never lets anything slide. In all things he contends it is mind over matter. I have seen him almost asleep in a chair and remarked on his tiredness, and his immediate reaction is, 'No, I'm never tired.'

"During his working days he also took a correspondence course on the advancement of his work in the mines. He contends you can do anything if you put your mind to it.

"His reading has been vast, from politics to war, and from religion to science and medicine. He spent a lot of time devoted to the St. John's Ambulance Brigade and I can remember a young child who whenever she fell or needed attention Dad was always the first person she came to for attention, no matter who was there. . . ."

"When my oldest daughter had her baby," Tom said, "it was a preemie. Would fit in a shoebox. She was married to a farmer, but things didn't go so well, and they split up, so I told Ethel I'd support her. She made her choice and I stood by her. I went to court and all, and we were awarded £2 a month for care of the baby. Fourteen years we raised him. I used to take the washing to her house every week, twelve miles on the push-bike."

1946–1948: Ethel.

Jan. 2, 1946, I took Billy and Jane to the circus at Blyth, and Billy Batey was here for dinner. . . .

20 February. Ethel came down on Wednesday from the W.L.A. after work to make arrangement for her marriage to Wm. Batey.

23 Feb. We had a one-day bus strike. On Sunday I took long walks with my children over many country footpaths and on March 2 I went to Morpeth with Ethel and she was married to Wm. Batey at Morpeth Registry Office. Annie Allison was bridesmaid, and we all went to Newcastle for the day, and I brought Annie back at 7:30 P.M. This was the poorest wedding I had witnessed in all my life. However, I was committed as a father to carry through. Ethel and Batey down on the 7th.

Saturday the 16th March I attended at Burt Hall representing our

115

branch of the union, then on to Blyth for the annual meeting of the Labour Party and here began my close connection with the Labour Party. Was idle to take a ballot for the union on April 10th, and when I got finished Mam and I went up to Saltwick to see the Bateys. Ethel and him came down on the 13th and there was some plain speaking done, and he stayed overnight. . . .

Easter Monday, planted father's garden with potatoes, worked all day and on the 26th was at Scotland Gate for a meeting of the Aged Mineworkers Homes Association representing my branch. I did the audit for the Nursing Association. . . . On the Saturday I went down to the churchyard and tidied up the family graves; this I had done for years and years. The next Sunday was at a concert given by the Doctor Pit brass band. . . . We had to go to the colliery to collect extra bread coupons granted to heavy industrial workers. Mam and the bairns left at 10 A.M. to go to Rothbury on holiday by taxi. Billy and I went to see Ethel at Saltwick and on to Rothbury later by bus.

. . . Mam went up to see Ethel at Saltwick for we had a disturbing letter from her the day before, but when Mam got there a baby girl had been born prematurely. After I did my first shift and had my meal I also went up to see her, and Mam went back Friday and did not get home until 10:15 P.M. The next day she did not come home at all. Got the breakfast and dinner over and Billy and I cycled to Saltwick (10 miles) and had some tea. Contacted Batey and remonstrated with him at his attitude to his wife with a small baby, got no satisfaction and we left at 8:30 P.M. and we were told not to go back unless we were asked to do so. But on Tuesday I went back again to Saltwick on the bike. Both were doing quite well. . . .

On Sept. 4th I got a letter from Ethel asking me to bring her home, so I went to Morpeth, saw the police before doing anything, then got a taxi and went up to Saltwick and brought Ethel and her baby home. Mam went with me. There was some words with the Bateys, but I was determined to protect my daughter.

At a meeting of the ex-officers of the 14th British Home Guard, it was decided that I be the secretary of the association. Sept. 20th took

116

Ethel to see a solicitor. Thursday Abe Reed, my mother's cousin, was buried at Choppington, father went to the funeral. The Ex-Officers Association began to eat away some of my time now, also committee meetings etc. Oct. 18th went to Brummell and Sample, Morpeth solicitors, with Ethel, and on the 19th David White died at quite a young age. Changed shifts on the 23rd and was at his funeral as an underbearer, and the next day started a course on music appreciation at Bedlington in the home of Mrs. Johnson. Band, Legion, classes and union became the order of the day now together with representing the union on deputations to the management. . . .

1947 opened with a new Era for coal mining, for on January 1, 1947 the Mining Industry passed into the hands of public ownership to be run by the people, for the people. We were at the colliery for a ceremony when the National Coal Board flag was unfurled and the plaque was unveiled on the side of the winding engine room. . . . The worst February weather in 50 years, and we succeeded in getting new piecework rates. Ethel went back to her home at Saltwick. March 17th a new conveyor started in the West Plessey Seam. March of this year was recorded as being the wettest March for 90 years. April 3rd our Bill cycled up to Ethel's home to see how she was, and on Tuesday he complained all night about a pain in his leg, so we got the doctor in, and on Wednesday his Mam had to take him to the hospital, and after examination they put a plaster on his leg.

. . . Billy still complains of pain in his leg, and never really had any sleep, so on the 15th I waited out of bed until the doctor came and I told him I was not satisfied about this leg and wanted something done about it, and after examinations he ordered Bill back to the hospital, and Mam went with him in the ambulance, and a cleaning operation performed for Osteomyelitis. I visited him Sunday slightly improved. Friday Bert Phillips, who had been appointed training officer, was at the "A" Pit, and through some mistake when he came to the shaft to be wound to the surface, he fell down the shaft and was killed outright and I attended his funeral on Tuesday. The following day Bill got out home from the hospital. May 5th, another Red Letter Day for mining,

we commence to work the five-day week, and there was much union activity about this time in which I was engaged. Monday 12th May I handed in my resignation from the Union Committee because I was not in agreement with it. 26th, Bill and I made a pen for his rabbit which he had got from school. J. Tuck died. Met Mam coming from the chapel in the evening and we went down to Cambois to see her uncle Ed. . . .

Ethel came down with Carole on 7 August, the next day was her first birthday. 9th, Mam and I went to see the International Ballet at Newcastle, and Ethel was down home for two hours. . . . Councillor W.I. Heslop died Sunday 24th in the Avenue, and on Monday my sister's only daughter Ellie had a baby boy at Berwick, and on the Wednesday we got word that she was gravely ill. Got word the following day that Ellie had died (age: 21), this same thing happened to her aunty Ethel in 1925, but Ellie's baby survived, the other one did not. And on Saturday we all went to Spittel and saw her laid away in the hillside cemetery just by the Great North Road, we were back again at 6:15 P.M. We gave up collecting the rents at East Sleekburn for Miss A.M. Coxon, her nephew was to take over.

Miss Coxon had been a dressmaker in Tom's father's time, and as a boy Tom had done yardwork for her. In her old age she made him her executor, and for his extraordinary services in protecting her interests during a squabble over her will she eventually left him some property. He was able to make some modest investments, which he discussed with me rather proudly. Part of his nest egg was lost in a watchmaking venture with his son.

8th saw me again as an underbearer at Jack Armstrong's funeral, he was at the Boer War and used to tell us about it. . . . Nov. 18th Ethel and Carole came and stayed overnight. Mrs. Hall came from Berwick and brought down Ellie's baby boy Alan. Ethel and Carole down, and Mam and I took them home. . . . They were dispensing food packs held for emergency by the Government during the war, and the miners were awarded a fair proportion of them. We paid 22 and

6 for each one. On December 8th Ethel's baby boy was born. . . .

Up again to see Ethel June 30th (1948) and she walked down the fields with me, said all was O.K. Saturday the 5th was at Morpeth and saw the optician and on the 19th got my glasses and paid £1–0–6. Thursday, I make this note, our first tractor came into the field at the foot of the garden to do the ploughing. Back on the 27th to see Ethel. July 4th Mam and I went to Jesmond for the annual meeting Tyneside Scottish. 7th July took my first mining lesson, as arranged by my father, and on Thursday Ethel was down to see us with baby Billy, and Mother accompanied her to Morpeth. . . . August 25th another Red Letter Day, Ethel came home with her two children, tired of trying to live up in the country with Billy Batey, so we had to reorganize ourselves to make accommodation for them all, which we did.

Leafing through Tom's diary, I noted that the situation with Ethel dragged on for some time. Barely two weeks after moving in with her parents she went back to Saltwick, but she returned frequently for visits, alternating with Tom's trips to see her. Once he and his wife missed the last bus and had to walk the twelve miles home. Early in 1949 another flareup took place, beginning with "a disturbing letter from Ethel on her husband's conduct," and after several more visits back and forth, Tom got his brother Edwin to drive him and Mrs. Easton to Saltwick where "we had a first class row but came away feeling that we had achieved nothing."

Throughout the spring, Ethel's visits continued once or twice a week. In June Tom bought a pram (£3–6–0) and walked part way to Saltwick to deliver it. Finally, in September, Ethel appeared again with the children and "this time she said she was not going back, was sick and tired of it all. On Sunday Mother and I went back to Ethel's home and got her clothes." Tom bought a new bed for the extra children and took out a summons against William Batey for maintenance. It was not until 1950, after various attempts at reconciliation, that the court took action: "I attended Bedlington Court with Ethel, and a permanent separation order was obtained, and Mother and I took on the care and guidance of two other children."

Eventually, however, Ethel was reconciled with her husband. Now a nurse in Morpeth, she wrote that she would be willing to talk with me but preferred that I contact her brother William.

1949, Tom's mother dies: *Mother was back in bed again with a bad leg, so I was up to see her for awhile, and it was decided to bring her and her bed onto the ground floor; unfortunately we broke the star glass in the door at the stair foot in doing so. . . . 10th of December, Mother was ill at midnight, so I went up and saw the doctor. Next day, quiet but fairly comfortable. Back to work for the night shift on the 13th, but I was up to Mother's at 11:30 P.M. Condition canny. Back again on the 14th after I got from work, seemed canny but quiet, and on the 15th was called from work at noon, but Mother had passed away when I got there. A grand old lady lays down her tasks. Supervised the layout, after we had got Dad away to Edwin's. . . . Mother was buried at Cambois churchyard beside her oldest son Robert and youngest daughter Ethel May Chisholm. Stayed all day and night with Father.*

1950, a long year: *Notes for one month—Thursday March 2nd attended the funeral of A.S. Thompson, a Legion member; on the 4th over to the Store Hall and played until 11 P.M., then slept at my Father's house to keep him company. On Sunday up to the Legion Hut* and put on a fire, then back to the welfare pavilion for a Labour Party ward meeting, then back again to the hut at Stakeford, when we practised till dinner, then we went to Bedlington for a rehearsal with the Dramatic players until 6 P.M. Weather was fine.

On Thursday 7th we were at Bedlington to play the musical items for the amateur play, "The Gathering Storm," finished at 11 P.M. The same on the next two nights. In the midst of all the other activities and the day-to-day work at the Pits, on the Saturday I managed to get into my (garden) allotment and planted potatoes, sowed beans and parsnip and a little lettuce. Still sleeping at my father's.

Sunday again at my union meeting until noon. Ethel's husband came in the afternoon with his car and took them all to Whitley Bay. March 16 was at the West End Chapel for the Children's Gala meeting, when we usually started to make our plans for the Children's Gala Day in the summer, when we had a brass band and arranged fancy dress procession for the children for which prizes were provided, a free tea and a gift for all children, also sporting events, so we usually needed about £200 to carry out the whole Day.

Saturday saw me back at the allotment and Sunday to the committee meeting of the Labour Party ward, and was elected its chairman. Tuesday 21st of March records that I attended Colliery Consultative Committee, and this position I held until my retirement in 1961, continuous. Saturday 25th George Whitfield died, on Wed. I attended his funeral. Thursday saw me at the absentee committee, another new venture in the coal mining industry, and on the 30th went to see Frank Hogg of Ashington, a friend of my father's, who held first class certificates in mining. April 1 was at Newcastle for a meeting of the Aged Miners Homes Association annual meeting. Next week: Monday canteen meeting, Tuesday consultative meeting, Wednesday first aid classes, Thursday Childrens Gala meeting, Friday jumble sale at the Legion premises, Saturday practise at Bedlington, then give a concert at night, Sunday Labour Ward meeting. . . .

121

From *Northumberland Heritage*, Nancy Ridley: "In industrial Northumberland, especially in the coal field, where more and more miners are compelled to change their way of life completely as the collieries close and the 'new' towns spring up, some traditions and superstitions linger on. It will be interesting to see how quickly the social structure changes, as in every sense of its meaning the mining community has always been a closed shop.

"Bingo has superseded the quoit matches, but the miner has the old affection for his brass bands. The Telly rules the household as at one time did the whippet, but the pitman of Northumberland still indulges in his love of racing pigeons. . . . The working men's clubs in some of the villages are palatial but have long since lost their original purpose which was educational. Vast quantities of beer are consumed at the club, but there is no more generous giver than a pitman. Outings are organized for old people and children, and when he has something left in the pay packet no appeal for charity is ignored."

"At the Institute, where most met to read the papers," Tom wrote in a letter, "we had a reading room which tabled all the papers we could not buy; billiard room, games room, dominoes, etc. No facility for females. We paid by colliery levy from wages two or three pence a week. We had a resident caretaker who saw to cleaning and heating and running the place. The colliery company provided a house for him, and they supplied all the coal to heat the place. It was always warm, with roaring fires in winter time.

"Later the Coop building was altered and they put a hall above the premises which held all the dancing for the village.

"In 1954 I attended meetings at Bedlington 'A' Colliery Institute and West Sleekburn with a view to the Institute function passing into the hands of the Coal Industry Social Welfare organization. A local committee was always in being to handle matters at the bottom, arrange billiard tournaments, see that the place was run properly, always with the injunction of NO GAMBLING, for teen-agers were half-members, and we went most evenings in my youth and furthered our education."

One brief diary entry haunted me long after I read it. It was simply this: "Geo Rutter, Bedlington Station, died on April 14th. He was taken prisoner by the Germans in a raid from my section in June 1916, and we had always been good friends. He had never really recovered from this experience during the rest of his life, always good, but very timid."

There were many George Rutters, men whose nerve was permanently shattered, whose zest for life was burned out in the blast furnace of war. What was it that made Tom different?

My father had agreed to let Edwin my brother come into his house, and a start was made to clear the house of some of my mother's furniture, and the furniture went to the salesrooms, and I felt very disappointed about all this. I had slept in his house to keep him company, but he couldn't face it any longer living on his own, so the move was made. Then I began to build the garage framework at Father's house for Edwin's car. . . .

I got my left knee crushed at work but carried on all day under difficulty. Although hampered by the swollen knee I went to County Hall for an after-care conference, had tea there and only got home at

7 P.M. Weather was cold but fine. To bed early to rest my leg, still bad in the morning but I still went to my union meeting till dinner time. Monday saw me back at work at 2:30 A.M., managed with some difficulty but I carried on with all my fixtures, band, welfare meeting and Labour ward committee. . . . I was called back to undertake the night shift at 5:30 P.M. as this man had been unable to come to work, and this happened to me times out of number, they always knew who could be relied upon to fill the gaps. Being regularly in the foreshift at 2:30 A.M. and as the backshift man did not arrive, I had a meal and carried on straight through until 5:30 P.M.

November 6, 1950, another sad accident to a young married man. Jack Tubby was killed on W. Face Low Yard Seam, tragedies like these were often cropping up in our working lives. Typical of another day of activity, I was in the foreshift 2:30 to 10:30 A.M., rested afternoon, at the baths meeting at the colliery office, 5:30 P.M. to the Church of England Men's Society meeting, then to orchestra practise till 10:15 P.M., then to bed to be up at 2 A.M. again. Next day at the Childrens Gala meeting, and the next, was at work 2:30 A.M. till 5:30 P.M., and I just state ''bed early,'' and I would need to be.

The rabbit: My son had always kept a black rabbit that he brought from school, and he was such a pet at the bottom of the garden, he called him Sweep. Mam went down to feed him (because Billy now worked days in Newcastle as watchmaker's apprentice), and she got a shock, for she could see two sets of eyes in the dimness of the hutch. On going to investigate, I found that Sweep was dead and beside him, a ferret had squeezed in and was having the time of his life.

He got out under my workshed, so I sent for the only man whom I knew kept ferrets, and he came straightaway, for he had lost his ferret and this was the chappie. He was still hanging onto the rabbit, so I

slowly dragged the carcass forward and the ferret with it, and we had
to pull either way before he would leave go. I had to bury our old pet
in the garden, and that ended the rabbit keeping as far as our family
was concerned.

That Christmas, I learned from a conversation with Tom, was marred by the refusal of Edwin's wife to let her daughter accept a gift from Tom's youngest daughter Jane. "We made no to-do about it but never offered any more gifts." This episode was connected to the family tiff over the mistakenly opened letter. Tom had asked for an apology from Edwin, which was not given, and the two families had remained cool. The two little girls, however, continued their friendship.

Jan 1st 1951, at work, this being always my job to go on New Year's
morning, none of my working marrows would accept this, which was
purely routine, to allow men to get into the pit for inspection and feeding
ponies etc.

Horses were used in Tom's pit right up to its closing in 1962.

Saturday March 3 the Pit Head Baths were opened by Sir James
Bowman. Monday Mar. 5th, New Era in our working days, we went
to work in clean clothes and came back washed, thus taking a tremen-
dous amount of drudgery away from our families, wives and mothers.
March 7th, attended my first meeting of the North Northumberland
War Pensions Committee, representing disabled persons. In this year
was sent as a delegate to the Blyth Trades Council and served with
the body for the remainder of my working days and even after that,
when I was made an honorary member. March 28th Jane goes to
Paris. . . .

125

Temple: "Generally speaking, the lot of the miner did not improve until the Second World War, when demand for coal increased. For example, wages of British miners rose steadily after the war and underground workers were considered to be among the elite of manual workers in the early 1950s. Side by side with such developments has been the provision of welfare benefits such as baths for miners at the end of shifts, slow to be offered in Britain since they were first introduced in 1902, but compulsory in Germany from an early date in this century."

A typical Sunday for me. Church at 8:30 A.M. Holy Communion. Union meeting at 10 A.M., put on the Welfare and Housing Committee. Dinner. Rested until teatime. Up to Stakeford for the Bedlingtonshire Miners Federated Board, back down to church and had practise on the violin with the church choir for a forthcoming musical service, then home at 10 P.M. and out to work at 2 A.M. the next morning. . . . Mr. Moon got my 3/4 violin on loan, which has never come back. . . . We had an anthem in the church with the orchestra at evening service, after which I walked my grandson to East Sleekburn to visit a one-legged pensioner for an hour.

"I don't go to church much anymore," Tom said. "I disagree with 'em on some points, though they are still supported by us regularly. I used to go to church three times a day on a Sunday, but now it's my day of rest."

Mrs. Easton still goes, however. He said he had explored many aspects of formal religion, including Mary Baker Eddy's writings, "but I gave that away, for now I believe religion is based on a simple proverb, 'Do unto others as you would have them do unto you,' and you can never go wrong."

"I was down in my parish church yesterday," he wrote me once, "where the flowers on the altar are set and provided by me. I was in the church choir when the first Canon died, aged 82 years, so was born 1828, and I have known every incumbent of that parish church in the whole of its existence. I left the choir when I joined the army, and the same vicar was there when I came back in 1919, when I had some doubts about religious matters.

"I did not return to the church or choir. The then vicar asked me one day why I had not returned to church (although my parents always did) and I said, Well I seen many of the antics of clergy since I left you. My own padre was in a communication trench with me the night before we had to commence the Battle of the Somme, and we had to take shelter from shellfire in an old refuge. So he said, I suppose we will be all set for the Big Day tomorrow. I said, Oh yes. His next remark was, The Tyneside Scottish are a Rough lot, but a good lot, and I am afraid I have not been able to do very much with them Religiously. But while I have not been able to do that, it may fall to my lot tomorrow to be able to administer their last rites.

"That is, (I said to the vicar), he would be able to control them in death. This dwelt with me for a long time, and I did not take kindly to it, so if you drop your Collar off and come to work with us, then preach in your spare time like the Methodist lay preachers, the Salvation Army, then we may listen.

"Ah, he said, the Bible records the words that every workman is worthy of his hire, whereon I said that this did not especially attach itself to the priesthood, no more than any other workman.

"So he did not bother me any more, but I have still continued to use the services of the church."

1951: *June 29, attended my first meeting of the managers at Cambois Primary School, and still serving in 1972. Also our Bill got his new bike and I am still riding this bike in 1972. Friday went along to the Welwyn factory and met the management on the question of my daughter Isobelle dismissed for taking holidays out of turn, and I told them what I thought about their action, but they upheld their decision. Sunday July 8th, Jim Burns came with the car and we went to the 4th Battn. Tyneside Scottish annual meeting and service. . . .*

July 14th Isobelle and I was off to the Northumberland Miners Picnic Day, North Seaton Colliery Band wins the band contest. Lovely weather. Later we went up to Corbridge for the evening. Thursday, Jim Bowman dies, a colliery blacksmith all his life. 29th, Alan Rowlands was badly injured at the Pit and died the next day. Sept. 17, A. Young died today, a coal cutter for many years. 24th, Tommy Todd (Wink) died, on the colliery all his life except for war service. Oct. 19th Geo Heslop dies in the Avenue, had been a colliery electrician all his life. . . .

I took my father home to his house for he was not feeling too well, went home and did my church books for I was treasurer to the Parochial Church Council. Nov. 29th Harry Reed and I went to visit Ralph Murray at his home, who had been ill for some time, and this was my first look at a television screen in a private home.

On Sunday Dec. 23 I was called to the Legion premises at Stakeford, totally destroyed by fire. Salvaged the music trunk that belonged to the orchestral group that used the premises. It was more or less intact, slight scorching only. I had played in this combination for many years and we had quite an extensive library. Luckily we were insured against fire and received £500. . . . Geo Laws, a stalwart of the village, died on 26th December, and on the same day a small girl got hurt in the Revolving Doors at the Baths building. Total wages earning in 1951 were £514-1-11.

128

William Easton, 1868–1952. *Jan. 15, my father had a bad setback and was never really well again. Fortunately my younger brother had taken his house over, so he had no real worries from that quarter, but I do record in my diary that from January 15 until April 11 there was not a day that I did not make time to go and see my father, who in the latter part was mostly in bed right up to that Good Friday night.*

After I had attended church I went straight up to his house. My brother and his wife were in the kitchen, and they said he had been canny most of the day, so I passed upstairs and sat down at the head of the bed, but he never answered my greetings. And on a closer look I found that he had passed quietly away with only me present. So I called my brother, and together we confirmed that Father had died. I called again Mrs. Erwin, that great friend of the family, and together we carried out the last rites, as was my father's wish.

So passed on a fine man, a life long total abstainer, nonsmoker, worked at the Colliery for 62 years, having commenced work at the age of 12 years, and walked two miles from Guide Post each day to do so, and back again. Followed through every grade of Pit Work, educated himself and gained his 2nd Class Mining Certificate, which enabled him to become a colliery official, which he held until his retirement when he was awarded his house for life and all his fuel requirements, with a small monetary pension.

Lifelong church man, of the C of E church, for many long years its warden, a good violinist who had always led the Family Orchestra, who provided most of the music of the village in years gone by, a man who went to the grave at 84 years with his own teeth in fair order and attached to anything in the village that was for its betterment.

1952, a highly intensive year: *At the Parish Meeting April 24th I was NOT elected so that was one duty less for me, although I had hoped they would have been pleased to put my father's mantle*

*on me, but apparently there were others who had ideas as well, so I
carried on with all the other interests I had. . . . May 15th was again
elected Parish Treasurer and on the Sunday was elected vice president
of the Miners Union. I was appointed to sit on the Divisional Welfare
Committee for the union. . . . 21st of August at the vestry meeting
was beaten by one vote for the church warden post. Made Vice Chairman of the area Welfare on the 27th, and on the 28th we had the
inaugural meeting of the West Sleekburn Over 60s club, when I was
made a committee member. . . . Jack Jobson, picksharper at the Pit, died
on the 24th December, another old village standard. This completes
the year of 1952. No loss of work due to sickness. Total wages
£623–13–8. Tax paid £53–7–0. Mam's Fur Coat cost me
£27–10–0. Brothers agreed to erect a family memorial stone in the
churchyard to cost £64. Another highly intensive year.*

One afternoon Tom and I toured the villages where he
spent his life, past the small red brick church "where all
my people are interred," past the house where Mrs. Easton lived as a girl, past the salt grass marsh by the River
Wansbeck, the Saltens, where a century ago some of the
miners met secretly behind the dunes to organize the first
unions.

"My father didn't go for that," he said. "Many didn't.
There were two chapels in the villages sometimes, and
they said if you were aping the owners you attended the
top chapel at the head of the row, and otherwise you went
to the bottom chapel. It was all pretty fixed: the vicar was
named by the mine owners, and the schoolmaster too."

Close to the Saltens was the spot where a ford, marked
by stakes, once crossed the Wansbeck: hence Stakeford.
("If you went at high tide you couldn't get across; you'd
just sit with your horse and cart and wait.") Once he
pointed to a flat meadow knee high in grass, the site of the

only school he ever had. And in a hedge close by, he showed me gray stones embedded in the soil: "Ye see that, it's not a matter of great interest and yet it is—it's duff coal. Dross. You got nothin' for small coal then, you see. It went through a screen and this was all dead loss. They had no use for it. All that was dumped. Our floors were that stuff on the bottom with great bricks on the top."

(Those red bricks, scrubbed to a shine every week with water and a few drops of milk, would be covered with oil cloth and then with worsted wool mats that the miners' wives tatted themselves from scraps. Tom often drew the designs for the mats in his house, and when he showed me one, Mrs. Easton pointed and remarked, "That's yer old topcoat in there.")

Across the road from the meadow that was his school we passed another meadow, where once stood the row of houses in which he was born. "Two streets of houses were there," he said quietly. "They all had gardens, some front and back. And there was an open gutter for the effluent from the boilers, the caustic soda and all, came down the side of the road, and every house had a little bridge over it. It ended out in the fields, just an open channel. In the back would be the wash houses and pigsties and the middens [earth closets]. We'd have a fireplace in the wash house so we could bathe there and wouldn't have to wash in the parlor."

Though the sea at Cambois was hardly more than a mile away, and though as children he and his friends played around the rocky beaches all day, most of them couldn't swim: the water was too cold and the surf too wild. The mines used to dump dross on the beach, too. "When we walked we went with bare feet, because our parents said, 'We can't afford to have you kick your shoes off your feet, you need them when you go to school.' We never had shoes on. After those days we had no time for play."

The streets of Cambois were empty, many of them lined by vacant houses or merely cleared spaces. Many of the people had gone to work in the new industries around the county and as far away as Newcastle. In 1913, he said, a million tons of coal a year was being shipped from Blyth harbor. Now the main activity there seemed to be a ship-breaking operation.

Tom's first home stood barely fifty yards from the mine. "It was Number Three house from the pit. I used to fall out of bed into the pit, mornings. You could hear it start. We went to work at half past six in the morning and we didn't come home till nearly half past four at night, and in winter it was dark, you see, we'd never see the daylight all the week. Sometimes you'd come home so weary you'd lie down on the hearth mat after dinner, still black—as they say, you wouldna list—and your mother would put a pillow under your head."

The mine was closed now. A long grassy bunker was the leveled-off tip, and the shaft was covered by a concrete cap. When we stood over it we could hear the soft rush of air from the empty chambers below us.

"Fifty-five was the year I went into political life," a letter from Tom began. "I was chairman of the Ward of the Labour Party for our village when our County Councillor was made an alderman in 1956, so a selection had to be made to fill his place. I was the nominee for my ward and also for another ward, Cambois. We had to go to a selection meeting to be voted upon, and I was named. I was well-known at Cambois, having counted my wife from there. I had no opponent in the '57 elections so I was

132

returned unopposed and never was opposed up to the time of my being appointed an alderman in 1969.

"It was hard work. I was secretary of the Labour group on the council and did all the correspondence. I was also treasurer. Worked three hours a night on it. There were 36 Labour members, and no pay."

"Northumberland County Council is the major local authority for the County . . . educating 90,000 children, maintaining and improving over 3,000 miles of road, as well as a host of other services concerned with social services, health, the fire brigade, weights and measures, and the promotion of industry and development of the New Towns, with a revenue budget of £43 million annually and a capital program of £13 million. The County Council consists of a Chairman elected annually, 27 County aldermen and 81 County councillors. The county councillors are directly elected for three years and all retire together. Aldermen are elected by the councillors and sit for six years."

Northumberland County Handbook

"Oh, the committees." His hand brushed the air. "I was twenty-two years on the war pensioners committee, chairman of that. Eleven years on the hospital committee. We worked with seven hospitals providing various services. This Christmas I'll spend part of the day at a hospital. We set up a Bedlingtonshire Old Peoples welfare group and opened some day care centers, where old people are brought by bus three days a week and pay ten pence and we give 'em tea and biscuits when they arrive, and then a three-course lunch and tea and a sandwich before they go. Put 'em on the bus and see them to their doors. They do all types of remedial work and hobbies and such."

Tom took me to the day center near Blyth where he puts in three days a week. There was a large common room with armchairs, a dining area, a fully equipped beauty parlor, and three entire rooms for hobbies, including a place where a local artist coaches amateur painters, a craft room full of basketry and weaving projects, and a pottery room complete with kiln which stood next to a fairly elaborate wood shop.

"Paid for by the county," he said proudly. He showed me the African head he is carving from wood when he has time to spare. Mostly we peeked in at doors because he didn't want to get involved in conversation with the people there. (I got the impression that if I hadn't been along he would have settled down to an afternoon of chatting, for everyone present greeted him warmly.)

In the crafts room we came upon a spastic youth in a wheelchair. Tom talked to him with easy affection, stroking his lank hair and gently hugging him. Later, in the kitchen, he crept up to the place where a couple of pretty dietician aides were having tea and threw a glove at them. "Who's that?" one said, "is that Tom?" He popped gleefully into view.

The Eastons were invited to a garden party at Buckingham Palace at the golden jubilee of the British Legion, whose gold badge he earned for fifty years of service. (He joined at the very beginning in 1920, when it was the Discharged Soldiers and Sailors.) The incident irritated

Tom: "It was a proper shambles. There was no provision made for the people. It cost me thirty pounds, and we had to walk from Trafalgar Square to the Palace. I was thoroughly disgusted with the national leadership, and I said so. They should have collected us to be presented."

"They can't keep him down," muttered Mrs. Easton.

"Lot of 'em tried," he retorted. "I was chairman of all the war pensioners in Northumberland County, to go on with those committees you asked about. Chairman of the disabled advisory committee for employment. For years chairman of the eastern area of the county welfare committee and the health committee. Been in hospital management till I was seventy-two, helped run nine hospitals for eleven years. Also had a lot of jobs in the mining industry. After I retired I just added on more work. Never sat down." He sighed and continued his litany. "Chairman of the school governors. Treasurer of the Saint John's Ambulance Corps here sixteen years. Local employment committee. Secretary to the Ex-Officers Association of the Home Guard till that folded up. Secretary of the Tyneside Scottish Association. Poppy Day organizers. And all the church jobs. I should write you a list."

The list: Northumberland County Council—alderman, secretary and treasurer of Labour group, police authority, fire brigade committee, highways committee, health committee, social services committee, selection and establishment committee, policy advisory committee, council-staff joint committee, chairman east area health committee. Area posts—Bedlingtonshire Voluntary Committee for the Handicapped, chairman mid-Northumberland and Tyneside District War Pension Committee, Northumberland Executive Committee for local government

135

reforms, chairman of the panel of the Disabled Advisory Committee, President No. 1 group, Royal British Legion; Stakeford branch secretary, chairman West Sleekburn Middle School Governors, Stakeford Poppy Day Organizers.

Also there were the posts in the union, which Tom joined in 1921: as delegate to the Northumberland Miners Council for years, he received the public exposure that led to his political career. And the church work: treasurer to Saint Peter's Church Council, church warden for a year, Church of England Men's Society, plus miscellaneous village chores.

"Needless to say," he added, "I have always been faithful to every cause that I was drawn into, attend all meetings possible or give satisfactory explanation for not doing so."

1953: *On the first of January I was at work 5 to 11 A.M., rested awhile and after tea I delivered books to an ailing ex-soldier and visited my two aunts on my father's side. . . . the 7th saw the pumping from our Pit put onto the new pumping column, which weekend after weekend, Saturdays and Sundays, had been built up from the Pit Bottom over 240 yards of it. Quite an engineering feat, carried out with little or no attention or fuss by the general workers, yet it was a system that could convey 600 gallons of pit water a minute to the surface. We had a demonstration of the self-rescue apparatus which was to be tried for a year at the colliery, each miner to carry this mask, calculated to carry him through noxious gases should an explosion occur. Fortunately it never had to be worn.*

"I was never in a disaster," he said once, "but we had one here five years ago, in '69, with ten dead."

Charlie Johnson, a close neighbour all my life, died in the Pit at 10 A.M., his parents and mine lived next door to each other for many years. We both joined the army in 1914, in the last 23 years he lived two doors from me. I was sent over to the home to assist in getting the body into the house, for he was rather a heavy man. Jackie Gleghorn died the next day, but as I was working 4 A.M. to 8 P.M. I did not get to either of these interments.

"There was no blacklung in our mines when we picked out the coal by hand," Tom said. "The blacklung only came when they started using machines, which dug into the rock and kicked up silicon dust. Coal floats on water; it floats out of the lungs. But rock dust is what makes the silicosis."

Coronation Day on June 2nd, winds and heavy rain swept the county and all outside festivities were impossible on this very important Day, but we held the Coronation Tea on Saturday in the store hall, when all the children had a grand time, and we had met and worked months to make this possible. All children got their coronation mugs and were tea-ed and feted. The Pits had a holiday, but I was at work 4 A.M. till 10 A.M. for essential services. The following morning was back at work at 2 A.M. when 36 miners did not report for work.

Wednesday July 1st, memorable day to us Tyneside Scottish, finished my work at 8:30 A.M., rest awhile, to the Welfare Building, prepare for the Area 2 Welfare Committee, my wife waiting on at the tea that was provided by the local committee. I was again elected chairman of this important committee covering about 14 welfare schemes from Dudley to the Wansbeck. . . . Saturday was Gala Day, prepared in the morning for the parade of children, however we ran into a thunderstorm which completely spoiled this, but we got through the day in a limited way. Having a look at my allotment I found bees had swarmed on my broad beans, saw the beekeepers and they took the swarm to their hives. . . . Saturday at work 4 A.M. to noon, Mam and girls to Rothbury by car, Bill and I follow by bus to commence our annual holiday. Three rooms for two weeks cost £6–10–0. We brought in our own food. The landlady cooked it. Sept. 1, Ethel takes up a new job at the YWCA in Newcastle.

. . . Sept. 26 to Oct. 3, attended mandate conference at Margate representing the National Union of Mineworkers. A hectic week. Here I met Seretse Khama, who was to be a very controversial character in later years, in the emergence of the African communities. . . . Took a wreath to Ashington for the funeral of Joe Auld, an ex-Tyneside Scottish member, before going to bed at 4 P.M. from foreshift. . . . Nov. 19th was made treasurer for the division of St. John's Ambulance and held this post until its disbandment. It was on this day that we installed our electric washer in the home. 26th Tommy Bradie's wife was electrocuted in her bath due to some bath heater.

New Year's, 1954: *In beginning this year, it is worth noting that there was a slight decline in wages. 1952 reached a peak of £623, but in 1954 it had slumped to £535 on which income tax of £32 was paid. But I start the year the same way as for many years, at my daily work at 4 A.M. when most of the village had not yet gone to bed, carrying on celebrations. Most mining villages never went to work on New Year's Day but maintenance had to be continued. Then my visits to my aunties in the evening, with whom contact was always made at least once a week.*

A blocked drain at the Legion HQ needed my attention the next day, and on the 8th was back at Aunty Bella's and helped to bathe the uncle, who had chronic bronchitis.

Jan. 9th, Mrs. Laws Bomarsund, a good church woman, died today, but ever since 1926 they were always remembered as the people who black-legged during the strike. The husband and sons came to the Pit with police protection. It was never brought up after then, against them, but it was always remembered by that generation.

Sunday 14th, Holy Communion, special union meeting to noon, then to the Federated Board of Colliery Branches when I make my report, and to end the day I visit my mother's eldest sister, age 84, who always smoked a clay pipe. . . . Tuesday 2 March Ted Thompson dies, an amputee from the first World War whose needs was always my concern, whose service was with the South Staffordshire Regt.

Saturday 20th Uncle Tom went along to Bomarsund to live with his son, he was my aunt's second husband and I always looked in to see him. Drew up his last will and testament and visited him on the 24th, had this signed and deposited. Joe Mordue, Ashington, old Tyneside Scottish, died. Attended his funeral and took a wreath. . . . April 18th Easter Day, Tyneside Scottish commemoration service when 80 attended. We also went to evening service at St. Cuthbert's parish church which houses our Battle Colour of the 2nd Battn. Tyneside Scottish. We had a grand day.

"Battalions might carry their Colours for half a century or more, and when the worn fabric was hopelessly frayed, they laid them up in the regimental cathedral and were issued new ones. The loss of a Colour was a disgrace so keenly felt that officers and men would unhesitatingly risk their lives to save what Rudyard Kipling once described as something looking like 'the lining of a brick-layer's hat on a chewed toothpick.' "
Washing of the Spears, Donald R. Morris

1954, the last diary entries: *June 21st, Tom Hepper, watch-maker and great friend of my mother, died age 81. Was brought out of the workhouse to be a tied apprentice to a jeweler and watchmaker in Blyth, so my mother used to tell me. She was a domestic servant* *before marriage and she used to feed him for he never got too much to eat.*

July 1st, down to Blyth Trades Council, when we had a German delegation present. Rather a strange coincidence on this day. . . .

"Oh, I work at it when I can," Tom said. "Starting on my third volume now, taking it up from '54 on."

He showed me a shoebox full of small memo books and pocket diaries, dog-eared and scuffed, one for each year. No two were alike, and the ledgers themselves appeared to have been picked up on the spur of the moment.

"I work on 'em in the evenings when there's time."

Aside from his many meetings, Tom was not basically a night person. Every day he got up at 7 A.M., made the fire, turned out a competent breakfast, did the dishes and then headed off on his various visits and projects, returning home usually by teatime.

"I read the papers at night, peruse every column, and I record the obits from my village. I have the *Readers Digest* for the international field, my son gives it to me every Christmas.

"We don't go to the films to speak of. We don't go out much at all. On the television, we're very selective."

He told me about a documentary he had seen that week, about a primitive Indian tribe in Brazil. I had seen it too, and had been struck by the casual presentation of frontal nudity in both men and women, a thing that could not happen on American TV.

"Beautiful, they were," he mused. "Those beautiful brown bodies."

Mrs. Easton, to me, "Yer in bad comp'ny, honey."

I announced that I should catch the next bus to Newcastle to make the last train. The two of them argued

140

mildly but persistently over which bus I should take, and Tom won, assuring me the later one would be in time enough. He had some more talking to do.

"People tell me nationalization is a failure in Britain," he said. "It's not perfect, of course. We get this house rent-free, which means we're ineligible for certain social services because of not being rent-payers. I don't know if that's fair."

On Britain's situation in 1975: "Why did they stop the tunnel to France? And we, who achieved the Suez Canal, achieved Panama, everything like that. But the shippin' organizations is puttin' up the protest. It could have been achieved, and of course the money woulda coom, the money woulda coom. This year they'll turn the corner in this country. Oil will change it within six months. I get the monthly bulletin from the National Coal Board, a sort of newsletter, and I keep up with it. They send you these covers to bind them in. Turning the corner, this is what Wilson is waiting for. The great burden of import-export plus inflation is on us now, but we know and I believe you know that all the Arab sheikhs are sinkin' millions of poonds into this country. What for? Because now they dictate to us, but you see, if oil flows from our own wells, then we'll be puttin' our thumb to our noses to all the sheikhs and all them sort."

On the immigration to Britain of Africans and Asians: "We haven't had that influx here. Maybe in Newcastle and Leeds, but not around here. It's a consequence of havin' a commonwealth of nations. They have a British passport. Can you see what that means? A British passport. They're the people who made this great empire, a great empire, nobody can deny that, they're the very people who made it, with the labors of their hands. Our young people just don't understand this factor."

141

As for the immigrants who go on the dole immediately upon entering England, he said they were simply telling the British, in effect, Now it's your turn to protect us. "The actual burden falls on the working man," he added, with a slight shrug of resignation.

The Third World is coming up now, he said as an afterthought, and he thought the Russians were showing remarkable forbearance about this new power alignment. "They've kept their cool," he said.

Tom wrote these **Thoughts** on the back of some war poems he copied out for me:

"There is nothing without flaw to the critical mind. Right, left alone, can die of itself. It can only survive by repeated assertion. . . . Gratitude is a thing of indifferent memory. Honesty in nature is non-existent: everything that grows strives to steal the nutrition of its neighbour. . . ."

"Some Great Impositions are necessary to the times, to do eventual good. With the gradual disappearance of tramps, laziness is quite in danger of becoming a lost art. There is no punishment so bad as the punishment that lasts for all time; no satisfaction seems so complete as that of getting one's own back. Peace has her enemies as determined as those of war."

"Money isn't everything, but in worldly computation it seems to represent about 99 percent of it."

"At one time it was considered a form of punishment to scratch out the name of the erring one from the family Bible. To attempt to do such a thing today, the difficulty would be in most cases to find the family Bible."

"Contented minds: In my youth you could go into any colliery village you liked and pick out scores of them. But go into a colliery village today, in fact go almost any-where, and you'll scarcely find one."

"What is best must ever be in contrast; give us the happy medium and we are content."

"Nothing lives except by tolerance."

Since the post of alderman had been abolished a few years earlier, Tom had held merely an honorary post, with access to the county hall and a lifetime invitation to sit in the council chambers, but with no voice and no payment.

"This is okay," he said. "People can't say I did it for the money. I've always worked hard. I'd say that the higher up you go the easier it gets, because after a certain point it's only a collection of what people think. But it's the guys at the bottom who do the work every time."

Last time he visited the county council, he noted, they all welcomed him and told him he was the kind of person that was needed. "Yet they were all keen to abolish alder-men."

A shrug, a smile, a mild snort of scorn.

"I have one aunty left now. I've seen them all in their last days, visited 'em regularly. I take her wood and vege-tables from my garden. I try to keep them all in contact: sometimes I take the bairns on a bus to visit their relatives and give their parents a little rest."

It was time to go. Outside, the rain had started again. Tom fetched my raincoat from the bedroom and I put it on, declining Mrs. Easton's offer to warm it first over the fire. Tom had slipped into his short jacket and cap before she noticed.

"Yer not goin' out?" she said.

"Got to take him to the bus stop."

"Out in that rain?"

I said I could find the bus stop easily enough; it was just around the corner. But Tom, with the calm, grinning tenacity of a bull terrier with his teeth into something, said he would take me there.

"You're sure," I said.

He grinned some more.

"Put yer collar up at least," she said.

He contemplated his wife of fifty years and six months. "I can get along without you, y'know," he muttered, and she laughed then.

Just before the bus pulled up to our stop he told me, "Write those questions, now. About the war. Put 'em in a letter and I can deal with 'em at my leisure."

In my letter I asked about July first once again: how much could he remember of the minutes in No Man's Land? Thoughts? Feelings?

"Yes, as we made our way over in the latter stages of the charge, men dropped all around like ninepins. Apart from machine-guns, the German artillery was also very active, great sheets of earth rose up before one. Every man had to fend for himself as we still had to face the Germans in their trenches when we got there.

"I kept shouting for my MOTHER to Guide me, strange as it may seem. Mother help me. Not the Virgin Mother but my own maternal Mother, for I was then only twenty years of age."

From another letter: "At those ceremonies at La Boisselle in 1966, when my experiences were broadcast, I said my life had been spared and given to be used in the interests of others, for which thousands of my Soldier Friends gave their lives, and as I sit in Becourt Cemetery in the quiet of the early morning, not a mile from where they were swept into eternity, I can find solace by visiting their resting place, line upon line of them, and always come out with fresh dedication to this end. For they never grow old, as we who are left grow old. " 'Age does not weary them, nor years condemn,/At the going down of the sun and in the morning.'/*I do remember them.*"

It couldn't have been later than 6:30 A.M. when I parked the rented car in front of Becourt cemetery. The woods around us were lush and cool, and the smell of new-mown grass filled the quiet air.

(I had arranged to meet Tom at the Somme for three days and had picked a time as close as I could to July. It was the first week in June, just before my return to the States, and the weather did its best to act like midsummer. The day before, in London, it had been snowing, and even the previous night had been cold enough for a wood fire at the home of the Sevins, a young family who were part of Tom's network. He had made friends with the wife's grandfather, mayor of La Boisselle, during the war and had kept up the friendship through three generations. In 1958 the granddaughter, Lisiane LeJeune, then eighteen, had spent five weeks at Stakeford with the Eastons as part of a student exchange program, and now, married and a mother, she had invited not only Tom but me as well to stay with her and her architect husband in Albert and be dined and cossetted as much as we would let them.)

It was a small cemetery, hardly a thousand graves, between the paved one-lane road and Becourt Wood, a pleasant copse of ash and birch and maple and elm, young leaves gleaming in the sun. Above and below the cemetery on the slope was thigh-deep grass ready for haying. The usual fixtures of Commonwealth War Graves Commission cemeteries were here: neatly trimmed cone-shaped cypress trees, a gravel walk leading to the little temple containing the registry book and a visitors' book, a plain granite memorial stone and, at the far end, the cross of sacrifice, in stone with an iron sword superimposed.

What I hadn't expected was the flowers. They were set in narrow beds along the rows of graves, linking the weather-stained headstones with bright streams of marigold, iris, pinks, tulips, roses, and what Tom identified for me as primulas, arabus, London pride and Saint John's wort.

"Becourt Wood was a hive in those days," he said. "It made a good communication line. This is just behind Tara Hill, you see. Over there is Tara, across the road, and that's where the Tynesiders started down into the valley."

He walked past the even lines of Portland stone graves. The ones nearer the trees had a heavier patina on their curved tops.

"That's Peter Walker," he said. (P. Walker, 4–6–16, age 30. For King and Country.) "And there's Geordie Hall. I'm looking for Ned Mason—ah, there you are, Ned. (E. Mason, 4–6–16, pte.) The fourth of June, that was the big German raid. Tryin' to get information about our Push. We retaliated on the 29th."

Whole rows of graves bore that date, 29–6–16. Some merely listed the unit, and a few had nothing more than "A Soldier of the Great War known unto God." These were, Tom said matter-of-factly, "fillups" added to complete a row. Sometimes the soldier's family had arranged for extra words to be carved on the stone: "Dearly loved."

"Sadly missed." "In loving remembrance until we meet—Father."

The Tyneside Scottish emblem, the Newcastle coat of arms with the Saint Andrew cross above, was carved on stones everywhere. There were other emblems, of course. Tom spotted one for the Durham Light Infantry. "Dirty Little Imps, we called 'em. They called us the Tin Soldiers."

We walked across the road to the gentle slope that was Tara Hill, an almost erotically smooth curve of light tan earth plowed and harrowed with a craftsman's care. On our left was Usna Hill, and before us was the valley where the British insisted on placing their troops, to be looked down upon by the Germans entrenched on the ridge opposite. That ridge, less than a mile away, bore a superb stand of grain, shining green and perfect in the clear light. The landscape, with its soft swellings and picturesque tufts of trees and spired hamlets half-hidden in its valleys, seemed at first a Land of Counterpane, especially under this blue sky with its cottony cloudlets. But later I decided that it had too much energy. As we drove for miles across Picardy, vast Kansas-sized fields stretching to the horizon, with the view broken only by the double ranks of elms that flanked each road, I felt the huge, dozing strength of this rich farmland. The elms had been pruned as high as twenty feet, giving them an oddly formal lollipop shape. Many fields were deep in ripe wheat which the wind riffled like velvet, in following waves.

It was absolutely impossible for me to relate this place to the ugly scenes of 1916. "Oh yes," Tom said, "it was a terrible sight. The trees were all just ragged stumps, and the ground was completely torn up. Wherever you dug trenches they left a white slash, because you come to pure chalk a few inches down."

One can still just see the herringbone patterns of white veering faintly across some of the plowed fields.

I had vaguely thought that all of northern France had looked like a battle zone in those years; the old photos showed nothing but shredded trees, unbelievably pocked bare earth covered with thickets of barbed wire and muddy ponds and the shocking detritus of war, a cratered moonscape where nothing could live, a place where even the worms died. And the villages had been smashed too, the ones you saw pictures of. The hamlets Tom took me through had been then merely a few wattle-and-daub walls with great holes through them, exposed cellars full of broken crockery and rotting potatoes, piles of rubble in the streets.

But once you got away from the Western Front itself, a mile-wide scar that meandered from the sea to the Alps, the countryside was amazingly untouched. Tom told me of marching up the dull, straight road from Amiens to Albert through a land bursting with summer. Over and over, the soldier diaries describe the buttercups and dandelions and poppies, the butterflies dancing above fields of bright mustard, the fluttery young aspens and vaulting elms and flowering chestnuts whose leaves barely moved in the brilliant haze, while around one, bees rushed officiously and flies hummed, and in the rain-freshened ditches frogs croaked. Especially there were larks. Almost everyone who was there speaks of the larks, rising joyously even in No Man's Land.

We drove to another vantage point close to the great mine crater. This was supposed to have been blown under the hamlet of La Boisselle, but somewhere along its two-mile length the tunnel went wrong, and the whole effort was wasted on a tremendous explosion two hundred yards off-target. A section of land around the crater had been left as it was in 1916, though an apple orchard had grown up among the zigzag ditches and ungainly grassy humps. Just down the slope was the former LeJeune farm, a stone's throw from the place where Tom had charged up to the German lines on July first.

"I want you to see Contalmaison, up the Albert-Bapaume road," he said. "That was our first objective. They expected us to go the two miles in the first stage, when we couldn't get fifty yards all day."

Directly across the path he had taken on that long day was a red brick farm house. A young farmer was steering a tractor through a hayfield. It was barely one hundred yards to the bottom of the valley and partway up the opposite slope, where the Tynesiders had begun their charge. At the point where Tom had tumbled into the German lines, taken over a dugout and spent two days and a night, there was now a modest memorial to the Tyneside Scottish.

And it was here that the terrible morning of July 1, 1916 really came alive for me at last. As I stared clean through the pleasant green hillside on that sunny morning, with the tractor snorting in the distance, and Tom standing beside me lost in thoughts of his own, I could see him on another sunny morning under the same sky with the same ridge confronting him.

And I could see him running, pelting down the slope through the churned earth and smoke and the screams and the mad juddering of machine guns and the roar that pressed against his face like a high wind. I could see him, his long face twisted, his eyes bulging, his body bent as though to duck the blizzard of steel and lead, while he walked as ordered, then trotted and finally—people dropping all around him—ran, ran straight at the enemy trenches, ran for all he was worth. And all the time shouting at the top of his lungs: "Mother! Mother help me! Mother! . . ."

We visited Orvillers–La Boisselle cemetery and the Pozières cemetery with its monument to 14,690 missing dead, many of them Tynesiders. Since the stone was carved, sixteen bodies have been identified, probably dug up by farmers or highway crews, but their names remain on the stone panels that stretch around the entire cemetery, rows and rows and rows of them.

We stopped at more cemeteries than I can remember now, and in each of them Tom had come upon some of his comrades in previous visits.

"Hi Donkin, how are ye?" he chirped, passing one stone. (Sgt. Henry Donkin, 33, Blyth.) "Aye, that's Harry, he was sergeant of my company. And there's one of my men (J. Price, pte.) and him, he was an officer of mine." (W.H. Furse, second lieutenant, 1–7–16.) "Two of my commanding officers are in here, and the other two are in the Thiepval memorial. Which I don't understand because they were all together that day. All four of 'em died on the first."

He found the grave of W. Lyle, forty ("an old man to me—he was one of the Lyle sugar people"), and farther down the line: "Somebody wanted to separate these two, for some reason or other, but the guy in the burying party told him, 'The buggers died together and they're bloody well gonna be buried together.' "

Many of the remarks in the cemetery visitors' book praised the maintenance work or commented simply, "Lest we forget" or "Merci à Eux" or "We must remember." A few said more. "My grandfather was wounded here." "My father fought in the Kings Rifles here 1916."

150

"Served with the Argyll and Sutherland Highlanders '39–'45." "My twentieth visit here, still well maintained." "Un ancient combattant, '14–'18."

A Welshman had written, "Poor bastards," and Tom didn't take kindly to that. "Bastards?" he growled. "It's insulting."

Slightly west of the territory where Tom fought was Newfoundland Park, at Hamel, where many acres of battlefield were preserved in memory of the Newfoundlanders who died in the terrible assault of Y Ravine, and a great monument of a caribou is automatically floodlit every night. We could see the corrugated remains of dugout shelters among the winding trenches. In front of the line stood a forest of the corkscrew steel stakes on which the British draped their barbed wire, and to the north, hardly two hundred yards away, were the German trenches. Shell holes were everywhere. It took us many minutes to scramble across what had been No Man's Land, grassy but still riddled and pocked and blasted after sixty years.

Later I talked to the caretaker's wife who lived at the edge of the field. "I cried a lot for no particular reason when we moved in here ten years ago," she said. "We found we couldn't sleep at night, we couldn't stay in the same bedroom, and we'd wander through the house all night, moving from bedroom to bedroom. We still can't dig in the garden. There are bones everywhere."

A Canadian veteran of the 1944 invasion of France walked around with us for awhile, and his discovery that the advance headquarters dugout was only twenty yards behind the front line stirred some memories in Tom.

"We used to have batteries to run the telephones, and the ground wire was attached to a pin that you stuck in the earth. When the battery ran low, you could sometimes

151

revive it a bit by wetting the earth around the wire. One of my boys was on the phone one night, and it got so faint he could hardly hear the guy on the other end, so he said, 'Why don't you piss on your bloody old pins so I can hear you?' Guy on the other end was a brigadier general."

Sometimes a signalman in the rear would set the phone close to a gramophone and play band music for his friends at the front. At a busy communications post a signalman would rig up a switchboard from empty cartridges stuck into some cardboard and would then stick wired-up slugs into the appropriate holes.

"I had to work the phone one day when I had been fixing my clothes, and I had some pins in my mouth, and afterwards I missed one pin, thought I'd swallowed it. So I went to the doctor, and he said, 'You again!' because I'd been in before with a boil on my throat [which Tom had brought to a head by a home remedy rather than have it lanced]. He said there wasn't much to do, but 'you should examine what you pass for a few days.' I said, 'No thanks. If the pin doesn't trouble me I'll not trouble the pin.' "

We drove to Thiepval, a stark domed structure 150 feet high that dominates the landscape for miles. It is a monument to the missing, the largest of its kind here. The size of the thing is staggering, its very scale somehow alleviating the ugliness of its proportions. There are sixteen huge stone piers. Each pier has four faces covered with stone plaques. There are ninety-six plaques on some faces, eighty on others. Each plaque has from 11 to 14 names on it. There are 73,357 names on the Thiepval monument. Since its erection 280 names have been connected with bodies found after the war. The rest are simply gone, erased, blown into bloody rags, drowned in mud, buried in lost dugouts, atomized by direct hit.

Two faces and more were needed to list the missing of

the Northumberland Fusiliers, of whom twenty thousand, or two-thirds, fell at the Somme.

"In my village the people were dead scared of the postman. If you saw him comin' down the street with that letter marked On His Majesty's Service. . . . Dead scared."

While I backed off trying to fit the building into my camera viewer, Tom talked to a workman who was grooming the already trim lawn, atwinkle with marguerites. In the middle of their halting, arm-waving conversation the man abruptly bent down and picked up a shrapnel ball which he gave to Tom. I hefted it. It was lead, half an inch in diameter.

"These used to burst about eight feet above your head," he said. "It wasn't much bother unless you were right under them."

Just before we left he found the name of his signal officer, the man whose tags Tom had taken from the body along with his papers during the excitement of the first.

"I shouldn't have taken both tags. You're supposed to leave one on the body. The man might not be marked missing today if I hadn't taken both. I always had a bad feeling about that."

He was also anxious to find the grave of a major he had served under, and in fact the next day we drove to Arras to look up the name with the War Graves Commission and eventually found the man listed under his original unit from which he had been transferred before the battle.

"They stay young, all those men. We went from one crucifixion to another, all of us together, but now they stay the way they are, they never age. I remember them so."

The first morning of our travels we had stopped in at a rundown estaminet along the Bapaume road at La Boisselle, the Café de la Jeunesse. Walking straight in, Tom

153

asked for Madame in his Geordie French, and a puzzled youth pointed the way through the bare little room with its wall calendars and makeshift bar displaying a half-dozen aperitif bottles. Through the rear door we saw an old woman, very fat, peering up from her chair with the querulous look of the newly blind.

She didn't recognize him until he caressed her hair and cheek and repeated his name. Then she began softly to weep. Her son had just died, she said, and now she was blind and crippled and soon to go, and the grandchildren were running the place.

For a half hour Tom sat with her, saying little. The grandson gave us a bottle of orange soda. She was eighty-seven years old, she told us. The café stood where the German second line must have been, maybe thirty yards up the slope from the point Tom had reached on July 1. In the end, they sat together without speaking, occasionally touching hands, in silence.

We went on to another estaminet, no longer in business, where the reception was much happier and noisier. Here the madame, a young woman with indifferently dyed blonde hair, broke out coffee and wine and sent her husband to find a friend who spoke English. We stayed there for two hours, Tom chattering in some relief to the English-speaking caretaker of the Newfoundland Park, a transplanted Newfoundlander, and also taking a glass of wine and even what he was told was cherry juice, but actually was a quite fine homemade liqueur. We had had no lunch and only a slice of bread and an apple for breakfast, so both of us fell upon a plate of sugar wafers that appeared.

From time to time neighbors popped in to join the increasingly hilarious circle at the table, and before we left Tom had been invited to come for dinner later in the week, towards the end of his extended stay with the Sevins.

Everywhere we went, he plunged into conversation with the people we encountered, carrying on from the first pleasantries, patiently repeating his French and gesturing freely. Soon the camera would come out, snaps would be taken and addresses exchanged.

At one cemetery he talked to the head gardener, an Englishman, and inquired about an old acquaintance on the maintenance staff. The man was produced, amazingly, and shambled up, staring, face gradually widening into a grin, finally embracing and kissing Tom no fewer than four times. They had met years before during one of Tom's vigils at the cemetery, and the man said through the interpreter that he had saved and enlarged the photo Tom had sent him.

Another day, looking for a particular section of trench, we trespassed onto a rundown farm with geese in the yard and a ferocious, growling chained Alsatian which lunged at us in fury. From the doorway a huge, scowling, sour-faced man watched us.

As we approached the dilapidated porch, the six-foot-three figure lumbered forward with great stiff Frankenstein steps.

"Maybe we should get back to the car, Tom," I said. "Uh, Tom! Let's go, Tom!"

I had my hand on the car door. Tom paid no attention. He marched straight up to the giant. And—to my horror —chucked him under the chin. Crooked his finger and tickled the man under his stubbly jaw. And started talking to him in his Geordie French.

Two minutes later the man was reminiscing about the war, showing us where the trench had run, and hauling out the dirt-crusted shell nosecaps, helmets and other

155

souvenirs he had plowed up. Every farmer on the Somme has a pile of these objects.

We drove to Bully-les-Mines where a former Sheffield pit lad ran an immensely successful café, hotel and night-club complex known as Johnny's. Here we had lunch and Tom weathered his first rebuff, from Johnny's mother-in-law, who said she didn't recognize him and anyway she couldn't keep straight all the old soldiers who came through there. Neither of us mentioned the fact that I paid for the lunch, which I was only too glad to do, considering all the meals he had given me. I never did learn how to give and take gracefully with Tom.

As we drove through the summer heat Tom pointed to various landmarks of his short, intense life in this valley. Here was the woodshed where he and his company had spent several nights: still standing. Here, in the cobbled town square of Arras, with its ornate Flemish façades and bullet-scarred stone columns, he had been billeted for many weeks in the sidewalk cellars: still there. Here was the place where the men got a rare showerbath, to which they were marched in only their greatcoats, puttees and boots.

It was evening when we returned to Albert, and that night we stepped across the street for an elaborate multi-lingual dinner with Mrs. Sevin's parents. By the time we got home the town hall clock was ringing 11:45 P.M. in its curious leaden voice: dink-donk-dink-donk, and the night air was sweet with the smell of grass.

We were up again by 6 A.M. and on the road shortly after. I had only a few hours before I would have to drive back to Calais, so I had decided to make a quick visit to Amiens Cathedral, which was so near I hated the thought of missing it. We reached the old city long before the shops were stirring and were able to watch morning sunlight streaming in through the magnificent transept rose window above what Tom called "the side door," and later we had coffee at a sidewalk café that was still being swept out.

Before returning to Albert, where I was to drop Tom off, we visited the Amiens museum's early history room, full of flint arrowheads, bronze swords and other evidence that even before 1939 and 1914 and 1870, there had been the English, routed by Joan of Arc, the Romans, the Nervii and, for all I knew, the Beaker People. On the drive back we didn't talk much.

Ways I saw Tom during those days:

*Before I arrived he had written that he would wait for me at the Albert town hall. I was nearly three hours later than I had estimated, due to a hard channel crossing and other imponderables. He was still waiting where he had said. I reminded him that I had told him not to wait but to meet me at the Sevin home should I be late. He didn't say anything, but later I felt that he had sorted out our mutual share of the blame and had forgiven both of us.

*He awakened at five, shaved with an ancient safety razor and a cake of elegant Pears glycerine soap unceremoniously applied to his jaw, breakfasted on tea, bread and an apple, and was so concerned with not burdening the Sevins that we went hungry rather than accept the proferred sandwich lunches.

*He tended to repeat his war stories with the various people we met. Only one, the Canadian veteran, showed signs of boredom, breaking in with a peremptory goodbye and fleeing. Tom, who had indeed been sounding somewhat ancient-marinerish, didn't seem to notice. But the stories were less forthcoming after that. He used to warn me that he might retell a few stories, but I always assured him that I had the same problem, so not to worry.

*As a middle-aged miner, I gathered, he was something of a terror to marrow and boss alike when aroused. One reason he went topside at the mine was that "I was too forceful with people," and once when pleading a case as a union leader, the manager called him a liar in public, and he went around to the man's office after and demanded and got an apology.

*After the war, nobody ever stepped on Tom Easton; he had been stepped on by experts.

*He told me of some decisions he made as chairman of the war pensions committee for the Tyneside district, but then forbade me to make them public. All I can say is that they showed a practical attitude, dispatch and a hatred of red tape and, whatever his own feelings about a man's service record, a total and unerring sense of fairness.

My time was running out. I drove him into Albert and let him off. I took off my dark glasses and put a hand on his sturdy knee.

"I'll be seeing you," I said.

"I hope so," he said.

I started away, and we waved, and then I was on the Bapaume Road and it was still morning, hot and bright, and I went past the Bapaume Post cemetery and the cemeteries at Ovillers and Pozières and the Sunken Road, and across the hills I could see the Aveluy cemetery, and Lonsdale, and Blighty Valley, and the Gordon Dump cemetery, and as I turned west to Arras I saw the little white-on-black signs for the Grevillers cemetery, and Warlencourt, and Gomiecourt South, and Evillers, and Boyelles, and Warry Copse.

There is a map of the Somme area on which all the British military cemeteries are marked with numbered violet dots. The map is simply riddled with them. Some of these cemeteries have four or five thousand graves apiece; some have only a thousand. The biggest is at the former military hospital site at Etaples, with over twelve thousand graves, and the smallest must be one of those grassy nooks you see tucked away here and there containing perhaps only five British headstones.

I counted 140 dots on my map of the Somme battlefield. You add another 100 or so for the Arras area. You can get additional maps of Ypres and Passchendaele and Mons and Cambrai and Poelcapelle and Armentières and the other places, and all of them are covered with these little violet dots.

EPILOGUE

One of the last things Tom told me before we parted was that he was being considered for the order of Member of the British Empire. But it didn't come through on the next Queen's Honours List, nor on the one after that.

He wrote me about it, bitterly. "These things just don't happen to people like me," he said. All his life he had watched the better-educated, the better-connected win honors and awards. Officers got medals for breaking an ankle while falling out of a bathtub. Veterans who had seen far less war than he were decorated and written about and memorialized. His long life of service, his unfailing reliability, his willingness to do the hard things that nobody wanted to do, his loyalty, his cheerful generosity—all seemed fated to go unrecognized.

Then, at last, in the summer of 1977, he made the list. Went to Buckingham Palace for the investiture. Basked in his local fame. Tom Easton, MBE.

Of course I was delighted. I cabled him immediately and wrote a piece about it for my newspaper. Yet at the same time, in the back of my mind, something rankled. Why did he have to wait so long? What if he had died at eighty? Or, for that matter, fifty? The debts of love should be paid quickly, quickly.

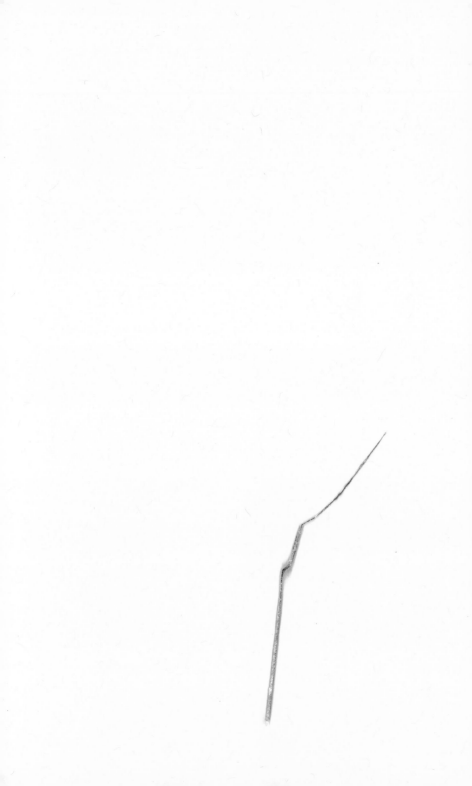